FROM WIMBLEDON TO WACO

Nigel Williams was born in Cheshire in 1948, educated at Highgate Scool and Oriel College, Oxford, and is married with three children. He is the author of TV and stage plays, and several novels, including the bestselling Wimbledon trilogy: *The Wimbledon Poisoner*, *They Came From SW19* and *East of Wimbledon*.

D1101026

From Wimbledon to Waco

NIGEL WILLIAMS

faber and faber
LONDON · BOSTON

First published in Great Britain in 1995
by Faber and Faber Limited
3 Queen Square London WC1N 3AU
This paperback edition first published in 1996

Printed in England by Clays Ltd, St Ives plc

© Nigel Williams, 1995

Nigel Williams is hereby identified as author of this
work in accordance with Section 77 of the Copyright,
Designs and Patents Act 1988

A CIP record for this book
is available from the British Library

ISBN 0-571-17439-6

2 4 6 8 10 9 7 5 3 1

For Suzan

Contents

Virgins over the Atlantic

'She is freaking,' said Ned, my eldest son, in a low voice. 'She is *seriously* freaking!'

Outside, in our front garden, my wife was doing the kind of walking usually associated with quarterdecks or condemned cells. Occasionally she would dart out into the road, raise one shoulder, Quasimodo style, and peer up and down the road. Then, muttering to herself, she would scuttle back to the front garden and resume pacing.

'It's only a *plane*, for Christ's sake!' said the middle one – Jack. 'I mean – planes don't fall out of the sky, do they?' Harry, the youngest, pulled his baseball cap over his eyes. He looked, briefly, rather round and nervous.

'Do they fall out of the sky?' he said.

'Never!' I said, brusquely.

As I marched down the front path towards my wife, I heard Ned say 'Except in South America!' He laughed coarsely.

Our trip to America had been in the planning stages for nine months. It already felt like something a lot more important than a mere holiday. The amount of time spent discussing it and the amount of money invested in it already suggested the kind of expedition requiring sponsorship from a major national news-paper. 'It is going to be,' I had announced in Pizza Express only the previous week, 'a voyage of discovery for all of us. We'll be finding out about ourselves as well as about a country that none of us has ever visited!' I had omitted to add that one of the things we would be finding out was whether Suzan was physi-cally capable of boarding an aircraft.

When I got close I could see she was in pretty bad shape. Her face was flushed. From time to time her upper front teeth would shoot out and nibble the lower left-hand corner of her mouth. At first, she didn't seem to notice I was there. When she did, she looked up at me piteously.

'Are 747s good?' she said.

'They are excellent,' I said.

Ned's face appeared at my shoulder. 'They've almost fixed the problem with the altimeter!' he said, with a grin.

Suzan glared at him and, once again, headed out into the middle of the road. The car I had ordered to take us to the airport was now thirty-five minutes late. At first I had thought that it might be doing her a favour by arriving late. Anything that came between her and the aeroplane was bound to be a good thing.

But she obviously didn't see it like that. She was now pacing up and down in the middle of the road, biting her thumb. This, I thought to myself, was how Anne Boleyn might have looked if her executioner had suddenly announced that he had mislaid the axe.

'Come on,' she was muttering. 'Come on, then, get it over with!'

Some years ago I went around boasting that I was frightened of flying. In fact, now I come to think of it, I *was* frightened of flying. I had taken what I referred to as my 'phobia' so seriously that I even paid money to a psychiatrist at Guy's Hospital. He had built a mock-up of the interior of an aircraft in a deserted shed. It consisted of two rows of moth-eaten aeroplane seats and a half section of fuselage about ten or twelve feet long. He strapped me into one of the seats and told me to look out of the window. He switched out the lights in the room. On the other side of the glass I watched a video of a plane taxiing to take-off, shown from a passenger's point of view. Meanwhile, from an enormous loudspeaker somewhere in the darkness, he played me tapes of an aircraft engine revving up on the runway. The tapes grew louder and louder. From behind me I heard the psychiatrist scamper round to the back of the machine. I peered into the gloom and saw him pulling on a gigantic wooden lever, which jerked me back in my seat at an angle of forty-five degrees.

'We're in the air!' he yelled. 'Look out of the window!'

When I looked out of the window at the video, I saw that we were already in the clouds. I stole another furtive glance in the psychiatrist's direction. He was bouncing up and down on his lever, giving it brief thrusts, first upwards then downwards, and then to the left and right.

'Turbulence!' he screamed. 'Nothing to worry about!'

Then he disappeared into the darkness, perhaps to make a cup of tea. But there was no simulated in-flight service. Instead, after a few minutes, he leapt out of the shadows and threw himself on the lever once more. This time he pushed it hard forward so that its tail pointed towards the ceiling and I found myself head-butting the back of the seat in front of me. Perhaps, I thought, he was trying to prepare me for those occasions when the pilot attempts to land by skewering the nose of the plane into a patch of soft mud.

'We're going in!' he shouted. 'Extinguish cigarettes!'

The whole thing, in my memory at least, was far more frightening than being in a real aeroplane. And almost as expensive.

But, looking at my wife, as she paced up and down in the middle of our street, I realized that I had never really been nervous of aeroplanes. Compared with her, I was a complete phoney. What I was watching, in our quiet street, about a mile north of Wimbledon Common, was naked, soul-destroying terror. Could this be something to do with the fact that this was the first time she had ever been in an aeroplane? I went out to her once again, put my arm around her shoulders, and steered her back towards the front garden.

'All it is,' I said, 'is that you don't know why aircraft stay up in the air. You don't know. And ignorance breeds fear. They told me about it on my course.'

'Why do they stay in the air?' she said, quickly.

I thought for a moment.

'It's the engines,' I said. 'You see – they're so powerful that the plane just lifts off into the air and … '

And falls flat on its face! I could hear my voice faltering. Why did the damn things stay in the air? As I was asking myself this,

3

round the corner of Holmbush Road came a large, black Volvo, which looked as if it, too, had designs on London's airspace.

I had seen the advertisement in the *Yellow Pages*, three days ago.

HIGH QUALITY CAR SERVICE.

LUXURY SALOONS WITH SMART DRIVERS.

Underneath, there was a picture of one of the cars, with a pencil sketch of one of the smart drivers. He did look uncannily like the man now climbing out of the large, black Volvo.

'It looks,' whispered Suzan, 'like a hearse!'

I could see her imagination once again, dangerously at work. '*Is that significant?*' Her anguished face seemed to say, '*Maybe he picked it for precisely that reason!*'

AIRPORTS AND FUNERALS OUR SPECIALITY!

WHY NOT COMBINE THE TWO?

The smart driver, who had everything a smart driver needs apart from a peaked cap, did not seem very impressed by his passengers. An ordinary English family going away for an ordinary English holiday. Three youths in sneakers, jeans and T-shirts, a tall, shabby man in glasses, and a small, red-haired woman, clearly on the verge of a nervous breakdown. Nor did he seem unduly worried by the fact that he was forty-three minutes late.

I opened the back door of the car and the children, as I still insist on calling them, dived into the upholstery, dragging their rucksacks after them. Suzan took one last, lingering look at the rockery, constructed for her by a man called Roger in the summer of 1988, and followed them inside. I started to haul the suitcases towards the boot. The smart driver stood a little way away, sneering at our luggage. I was just about to ask him whether he had a back injury of some kind when he said –

'There are five of you!'

I thought this uncommonly perceptive of him. There *are* five of us. Five mats on the table at dinner. Five tickets on Virgin Atlantic flight 007 to Los Angeles (*which departs in about an hour*). Five –

'I can't carry five!' said the smart driver.

In the back I could see Suzan getting ready to scream. It's *important*, I thought to myself, *to keep calm*.

4

'Why,' I said, in a light voice, 'don't you get into the car, and we can discuss this.'

Preferably while driving towards Heathrow at 90 mph.

The smart driver moved slowly towards the driver's seat. As he did so he produced a mobile phone from the upper pocket of his smart jacket. He started to talk to someone called Clive.

'Clive!' he said. 'Clive! There are five of them!'

He said this in a way that made us sound like people who had designs on his virginity.

'Clive, it's Ken here!' he went on. 'There are five of them, Clive!'

Suzan leaned forward over the passenger's seat.

'One of them,' she said, 'is a little child! He is sitting on my knee!'

'I am!' said Harry.

He heaved himself up on top of her. Harry is nearly thirteen. He weighs in at about six stone. He has asked me to say that, in the opinion of many, he performed well as the captain of the third XV rugby team at King's College Junior School, Wimbledon. I could hear Suzan gasp for breath under his weight as the smart driver continued to talk to Clive.

'He is only a baby!' she said. 'He is an infant! He doesn't count as one!'

People in our family are always saying things like this about Harry. I do not know whether this will come back to haunt and torment him in later life. He seems cheerful enough at the moment.

'He's tiny!' Suzan went on. 'Look! Look! He is minuscule!'

There was a definite satirical edge to the way she said this. I could see she was getting ready to zap the driver on the back of the neck with her hand luggage.

'While we discuss this,' I said, 'why don't we drive? Because' – I lowered my voice, and met his eyes – 'we are not going to get out of this car. We have a plane to catch.'

As far as I could gather, Clive seemed to be on our side. Perhaps his drivers were always ringing him up with little psychological problems.

A customer has a ring through his nose, Clive, what should I do? Clive, there is a Japanese here who wants to go to Euston station, what do you think? Is it safe? Clive – What does it all mean, Clive? Drive here, drive there … Clive … Are you listening to me, Clive?

Still talking, the smart driver put the car in gear and we moved off, slowly, down Holmbush Road.

'Suppose the police catch me!' the smart driver was saying to his mobile phone.

Jack inserted his face between the two front seats.

'Are you wanted for a criminal offence?' he said.

The smart driver ignored this remark.

'The police could stop me,' the smart driver went on into his mouthpiece, sounding, I thought, a little pathetic, 'and there would be five people on board!'

Clive was talking him down. We were already out on to Putney Hill. Whatever he was saying – it seemed to be working.

I know they're ungrateful. I know they don't care about you as a person. I know they don't appreciate you, Ken. But I care. I care that you're smart. Just drive them there, Ken. Just this once. For me. Go on. Please. You know you can do it, Ken. Please.

Ken was breathing more slowly. He seemed calmer. Perhaps Clive had put on some special tape – a deep, low, serious voice that helped him back from the brink at times like this. As I watched him, out of the corner of my eye, not daring to move in case he suddenly braked and threw us out into the road, his eyes acquired a glazed, indifferent expression – and he increased the pressure on the accelerator.

'Heathrow,' I said softly, 'Heathrow Airport.' I could not resist adding ' – It's down the M4.'

He did not, as many other drivers might have done, tell me that he knew where Heathrow Airport was, thank you very much. He had had his moment. Now he was all mine. When he responded, his voice had an automatic quality. He sounded like a man under hypnosis.

'How would you like to go?' he said.

'Well, by car would be nice!' said Jack, from somewhere in the back. But fortunately Ken did not hear him. He was in obedience

6

mode. He was, once more, a fully equipped, ready to go, state-of-the-art, smart driver. In case he might once again realize he was carrying the Williams family, and not some executive off to a red-eye meeting, I kept my voice very soft and sweet and low as I said –

'Left at the lights! I'll tell you the way!'

We went by a route of which I am particularly fond.

Left on to Gwendolen Avenue from Putney Hill. Left on to the Upper Richmond Road, right on to Priests Bridge and into White Hart Lane, left on to the Mortlake Road, right by the brewery and then right up to Chiswick Bridge. Left along Hartington Road, right over the railway bridge and then left on to the M4. The sun shone on English gardens stocked high for summer, past the brown Thames ribbed with tides, past cricket pitches, football fields and calm, suburban house fronts.

Suzan was looking, longingly, at every lamp-post we passed. There were moments when I thought she was about to leap out of the car and chain herself to one.

'It looks lovely, doesn't it?' she said.

'Home always looks lovely,' I said, 'when you're leaving it.' She gave me a sharp look.

And then we were turning off the motorway towards the airport.

As we drove up the approach road a huge jet roared up from behind one of the airport buildings, its nose pointed jauntily at the clouds as it clawed its way upwards against the forces of gravity. Suzan looked at it, flinched, then looked down at the floor of the car. A moment later her eyes flicked up and she was scanning the maze of service roads in search of ambulances, fire engines and the kind of field hospital that comes in handy when a jumbo jet explodes in mid-air or drops like a stone on to the roof of Terminal 1. The fact that the aircraft was climbing steadily out of her frame of vision did not seem to reassure her.

In the months before our trip to America, quite a few people had been surprised to learn that she had never been in an aeroplane. They would not have been surprised if they had seen her now. What was extraordinary was that a person like this should be anywhere *near* a major airport, let alone attempt to board a 747 and take an eleven-hour flight to Los Angeles. Would she run amok in the departure lounge? Would she, as one celebrated rock star was said to have done, suddenly rise from her seat as we taxied out to the runway, and yell 'This plane is going to crash! I know it! I must leave now! You must let me go!'?

The one thing I could not imagine her doing was going quietly. Perhaps I should have brought some kind of restraining garment. Perhaps I should have slipped something in her orange juice at breakfast.

'Where's the aeroplane?' she said, grabbing at my sleeve, as I dragged the cases towards the check-in desk. 'Where do we go now? Where is it? What's happening?'

I wondered, as we joined the queue at the desk, whether fear was not at the heart of our taking this journey. Whether fear was the reason I had stayed away from America for so long. People had been pretty surprised by the fact that none of us had ever been to America.

'Never been to America!' they'd say. 'Never been to *America*!' As if there was something wrong with us. 'Why do I have to go there?' I would reply. I don't think anybody was really convinced by my 'little England' pose. There had to be some darker reason for my prolonged absence from the place. What was so scary about America, though? After all, it was just a *country*, wasn't it? Like Switzerland, or Tunisia, or Greece? Was it the people? Was that it? Were Americans scary?

They were certainly different. But why? As we dropped our suitcases at the desk and, with that curious feeling of lightness that precedes climbing on board a commercial aircraft, wandered through to the departure lounge, I thought about Americans I had known.

There was the plump, middle-aged woman who I had helped to make a transatlantic call in Paris. She had wanted to speak to her son. She gave me a smile of utter sweetness as I wrestled with the French operator, and when I handed the phone to her when we got through, she said, without blushing, 'Hi honey! It's Mom! I love you darling!' All this, within *earshot*, was followed by another sweet smile in my direction which implied that I was doing the right thing by eavesdropping on a private conversation – indeed, so proud was she of her son and her love for him that if I tried to wander off she might well have grabbed me by the scruff of the neck and yanked me back so that I could appreciate how real and true and genuine was the love of an American mother for her son. I grinned then. She said – 'It's six in the morning in Philadelphia. He's just woken up.'

I saw Philadelphia as she spoke – a huge sprawl of clean, neat houses where people were not ashamed to say they loved each other.

There was the American who had come to our house only last week. He was wearing white jeans and he was immaculately tanned.

'You will love California,' he said, as if we had just bought it and he was wrapping it up for us to take home. 'It is exquisite!' There was the American publisher who had been in Vietnam and who had said, 'My worst moment wasn't when some idiot from West Point told me to walk down a path in the jungle – you never did that. My worst moment came when I was in Vietnam Veterans Against the War and a sixteen-year-old boy spat at me and called me a coward.' There were publishers who wrote me pleasant letters of rejection, telling me that my novels were 'too English'. And then, of course, there was President Clinton. He was an American.

Many US presidents have turned out to be a great deal less reliable than they look. But Clinton has raised the status of the office to new heights of improbability. It's the way he always looks as if he has just come from a rather good lunch – even at nine in the morning. It's that slight smile that plays on his lips, even when he is imparting bad news, that makes me suspect that at any moment he is liable to switch his eyes away from the press corps, stare straight into the camera, and address the watching nation thus: 'Eat, shit, sleep! What does it all mean?'

There was John Wayne and Leonard Bernstein. They were both Americans. They had that in common. Since they had – as far as I could work out – absolutely nothing else in common whatsoever, if I thought hard about the two of them, imagined them side by side or sitting at a table over a bottle of wine, I might gain some insight into American-ness. The trouble was I just could not picture John and Leonard together. Nor could I separate Lennie from his white tie, tails and conductor's baton, and John, even when supposed to be in immediate proximity to Bernstein, was always wearing boots, spurs, chaps and a gigantic cowboy hat.

'It's boarding now!' Ned was saying.

The flight had been delayed by an hour. I was staring at Suzan.

'Right,' she said, her jaw firmly set, 'let's get it over with.'

She gave a short, merciless laugh.

'At least,' she went on, 'we'll all go together when we go.'

I wasn't sure whether this was entirely true. If there was an accident, there was no guarantee we would all die. Some of us might get off scot-free. Some might be only maimed for life. But I thought it best not to get into a detailed discussion on the subject.

'In the Venezuelan crash,' Ned was saying as we trooped through to the next embarkation lounge, 'one man was thrown thirty feet from the plane. He was okay. He lost a leg, but he was okay!'

I think he was trying to cheer her up. All of us were worried that she might actually die of fright before we got into the air. But she was no longer listening to us. Clutching her hand luggage like a small girl who has been sent against her wishes to a distant boarding school, she stumped towards the plane.

'Mid-class tickets!'

This was us. I looked down at my hands and discovered that the palms were damp with sweat. Perhaps, as so often happens with married couples, one was expressing what the other was feeling. Perhaps I was the partner who was really scared. I thought again about my motives for going on this journey. We are all frightened of something, I said to myself, and we probably travel in order to try to escape it. Deep down, I decided, as I struggled on to the 747, I was terrified of the United States. That was why I was going there.

2

Five go to LAX

When I was young I thought beautiful women had to have blonde hair, slim hips, long legs and regular features. Since turning fifteen I have never expected the women in my life to conform to such absurd stereotypes.

Apart, of course, from air hostesses.

An unusual-shaped air hostess does not inspire confidence. I remember thinking on an Air Cubana flight to Havana in 1985, *'If they can't afford women under fifteen stone, what chance is there that they've bothered to service the engines?'* The Virgin Atlantic hostess did not score very high marks. For a start, she insisted on looking like a real woman in a rather silly costume. Secondly, she paid far too much attention to Suzan. Unlike the ones in the adverts for other airlines, she did not hover over my left ear adjusting my pillow, wafting Estée Lauder in my nose and saying things like 'I Taiwanese girl. I great way to fly.'

She was, of course, like most of the other people on the plane, British.

There seemed to be only one American in the immediate vicinity, and Suzan had got hold of him. He was from San Diego, he said. He'd been to England for a genealogical conference. 'How fascinating!' said Suzan brightly, as we taxied out towards the runway. 'How *fascinating!*' He seemed surprised at the intensity of her interest. Had he said he was an international refuse disposal operative she would have approached him with equal keenness. Anything that took her mind off the fact that we were about to be thrust into the upper atmosphere was welcome. She shot a quick glance over her shoulder and threw herself into a discussion of genealogy with remarkable *brio*. I watched her with admiration. She was clearly about to make her last encounter on this planet a meaningful one.

Unfortunately, as soon as we got into position, the man from San Diego whipped his face mask on, slipped off his shoes and, in seconds, appeared to be fast asleep. Suzan turned towards me. Perhaps she was going to engage me too in a discussion in genealogy? Instead, she said –

'It's now!'

'It is,' I said.

'These planes are sort of … new, are they?' Suzan was saying.

'Very new,' I said. 'Fresh off the assembly floor.'

Suzan shivered.

'But they have been tried out *before*, haven't they?'

'Oh, absolutely,' I said. 'They put them through very, very stringent tests.'

'Tests for what?' she said, brusquely. 'What tests? For what?'

Before Ned could fill her in on the dodgy ailerons, the substandard undercarriages and the fallen-off-a-lorry automatic pilots supplied to unlucky transatlantic flights by unreliable suppliers, the engines were up to speed and we were charging down the runway in a manner that suggested there was no way out of this but up. Suzan gulped. Ned winked across at me from his seat. Harry pulled his baseball cap over his eyes. Jack buried himself even deeper in his book. I found I was gripping the armrests quite hard. We were going faster, faster, faster …

We were in the air. The man from San Diego stirred slightly under his mask. Suzan peered across at the opposite window. We were climbing quite steeply, then banking to the left across London.

Suzan seemed, suddenly, rather calm. I sneaked a look at the man from San Diego. Now that I knew I was going to America (and up until this moment I had not been entirely certain of the fact), he looked different. Perhaps America was already exerting its spell on him, making him do all those strange American things I had never, until now, been able to see. I couldn't have said quite why he was different. The aircraft had levelled out. The 'no smoking' signs were off. We were entering the limbo of international flight. I looked at the man from San Diego again. I looked at him many times over the next eleven hours as we hung, apparently motionless, more than thirty thousand feet above ground level. I watched him refuse all offers of alcohol. I watched him go to and return from the lavatory four times. I watched him eat aircraft meals and behave politely to the hostesses. But he never gave up his secret at any time during the journey. I'd like to think of him as my first American. But my first real American, the man who for me set the tone of my encounter with that extraordinary country, was the Immigration Official who gave us our thirty-day licence to stay when we staggered off the plane a very long day later, into the warmth of a Californian afternoon.

He was wearing a khaki shirt decorated with some kind of epaulettes, and from the moment I saw him I was impressed by the glamour with which he managed to invest the simple act of opening a passport and peering into it.

'Wasn't he in *Diehard* 2?' Harry said to me as the five of us headed for Baggage Retrieval.

'I don't think so, darling,' Suzan said, 'I think he just works in the airport.'

'I'm sure he doesn't just work in the airport,' Harry said. 'I think he probably acts in his spare time.'

I knew what he meant. As we went out of the airport towards the USA, which for the moment consisted of a few palms behind some plate glass windows, I found it almost impossible to believe that all these Americans were simply waiting for taxis, selling cold drinks or bumping into one another on their way to the terminal. I had the strong impression that they were all engaged in some form of promotional activity. When the bus arrived to take us to the car hire depot, the driver did not look at all like an English driver. He did not look as if he had just come from a six-hour wait in a hospital out-patient department. He was young, he was glamorous, he was mustachioed. He set about the business of stacking our suitcases on the top of other suitcases as if we were about to mark him out of ten for enthusiasm, courtesy and sheer skill in the baggage-packing department. When we were all on board the bus he looked round, counted us all up, and rushed to the steering wheel as if he had been waiting all his life for the chance to drive piles of suitcases and four jet-lagged families the three-quarters of a mile from LAX to Airport Boulevard.

At the Hertz desk – my third real American (and they were coming so thick and fast now that at any moment I expected them to blur into each other and become the same kind of grey, formless mass you might find on an English underground station) was even more articulate, excited and passionately engaged in what seemed, at first glance, to be a completely mundane job. She punched her computer keyboard, she telephoned out to other equally enthusiastic Americans, and threw herself into my service with the keenness of a sea lion that has sighted fish.

'I can get you a deal for $150!'

She seemed pleased that she had saved me money.

In 46 years in the United Kingdom, I could not recall anyone, from shop assistant, through builder, to accountant or solicitor, who had ever seemed pleased at the prospect that he or she was going to save me money. This woman seemed ecstatic at the prospect. I could not believe that what she was going to do for me would stop at car hire.

When the transaction was completed, she changed as irrevocably as Ireland on the eve of Easter 1916. She threw me a piece of paper on which was written what looked like the kind of contract exchanged by high profile city lawyers, and said something I completely failed to understand. As I goggled at her she said it again. 'Limtedlibilladywaiverd'yoowarn'idd?'

All I could pick up from what she had said was that I was in a land where people encouraged each other to make free choices. I was too gobsmacked by the amazingly unconditional nature of her question to ask her what it was she was asking me whether I wanted. It seemed too pathetically English and small to interfere with such a powerful moment any more than one absolutely had to.

'I'll have it,' I said, 'whatever it is.'

I didn't actually say 'whatever'. I said (I was rather proud of this) 'waddever'. I was not only among Americans, talking to them, having my passport stamped by them, hiring cars from them, I was learning to talk their brave, frightening argot. I had only been here five minutes and I was feeling like an American.

'You got it!' she said. She was black. But I've only just remembered that. She was more American than black. I thought this was absolutely terrific. If my ancestors had taken her ancestors on a nightmarish six-month trip from Senegal to Charleston Bay via Liverpool, she showed no indication of being aware of the fact. As far as she was concerned – history was history. She was behind the Hertz counter hiring out cars and doing it good. I was doing it good too!

'*I hire cars good*,' I said to myself, and with a new spring in my step I turned back to my pathetic English family. They were sitting in a heap on a sofa in the far corner. I felt sorry for them. They didn't yet know how to look a black American woman in the eye and say 'I'll have it – whaddever it is' when she offered them a 'limtedlibilladywaiver'. They would learn, given time … although, looking closely at them, I wasn't entirely sure they were up to this huge, exciting country.

'Where is it?' said Jack.

'It's right out there, son,' I said. 'Let's go get it!'

They looked at me oddly as we trudged out into the baking afternoon. I walked with a Texas Ranger's stride, the suitcases bumping at my legs as, with the poise of Clint Eastwood and the sulky charisma of Marlon Brando, I moved to the big Ford Aerostar and opened the wrong door.

'I hope for Christ's sake,' Suzan was saying to Ned, 'he knows where he's going.'

'I know,' I said, 'I've looked it up.'

I climbed into the driver's seat.

'You take the freeway north,' I said, my Texas accent no longer simply in my head, 'and then head west for Hollywood!'

None of them seemed very impressed by this. Jack was droning on about the time I had, apparently, got them lost on a hill somewhere in the north of England. Suzan was saying, to anyone who was prepared to listen, that the LA freeway was one of the most dangerous road systems in the world. When you got on the freeway, she said, people drove straight at you from all directions. If you didn't get out of the way they shot you. Sometimes they shot you just for the hell of it. I told her she was confusing America with the movies. She said, as far as she could see so far, it was exactly like the movies. That, she went on, was presumably why I was sticking my bum out as I walked, trying to look like something out of *Gunfight at the OK Corral*.

'Don't hassle me, OK!' I said with a Bronx twinge to my voice. 'Don't give me grief! Shut up and let me think!'

Before she had time to ask me which movie I thought I was in now, I grabbed the ground plan of Los Angeles from the pocket of my jeans, and for the tenth or fifteenth time since leaving London studied it closely.

As far as I could tell, it was an ideogram, rather than a serious attempt to convey the geography of one of the largest cities in America. For a start, all the roads seemed to run parallel to each other or head straight into each other at right angles. This was clearly, even for a race as ingenious as the Americans seemed to be, completely and utterly impossible. The other thing this crudely schematic diagram did – it seemed unfair to dignify it with the word 'map' – was to suggest that some of these impossibly straight roads went on for miles and miles without bothering to change their names. There was a road called Wilshire Boulevard that, if the map was to be believed, went on for about as long as the motorway from London to Dover.

The other thing that puzzled me was that the place didn't seem to have a centre of any kind. It had been around for over 100 years. Surely they had had time to set out a paved area and slap a cathedral somewhere in the middle of it. Where was the railway station?

It was certainly big. It seemed to be about the size of Wales as far as I could see. It went north, it went south, it went east – the only thing that stopped it going west was the Pacific ocean and, as far as I could make out from the map, it had done as much as it could in that direction short of plunging itself into the surf. I caught sight of names that were vaguely familiar: Hollywood; Venice Beach ...

Jack was looking over my shoulder.

'What you've got to avoid,' he said, 'is South Central. Black geezers just leap out at you with flame throwers, apparently.'

'The riots,' I said, 'are over. Anyway – people only riot when they are provoked.'

Ned said he thought they probably rioted whenever they felt like it. Suzan said, could we stop talking about riots please? We should drive only on major roads, she said, and if we saw anyone who looked as if they might be trying to start a riot, we should accelerate away, as fast as we could, in the opposite direction.

'Until we reach the freeway!' said Jack in a satirical tone of voice.

There was only one person out on Airport Boulevard, but she looked as if she might well be in the throws of trying to get a riot together. She was probably, I decided, dropping round to a few friends to see if they could rustle up a few flame throwers. She was a black woman of about fifty with an alsatian dog on a long lead. She was carrying a grubby plastic bag.

'Drive past her!' cried Ned, in a satirical tone of voice. 'Drive on!'

'There are probably more of them!' said Jack. 'Behind the wall. Hiding!'

He laughed. So did Ned. Harry's eyes grew round.

It had looked, as maps do, fairly simple. All I had to do was find one of the long straight roads going north from Airport Boulevard, and sooner or later I would hit a road going west towards Hollywood. Our hotel was in west Hollywood. The trouble was, although I knew I was on Airport Boulevard (there were gigantic green signs saying AIRPORT BOULEVARD everywhere), I wasn't sure whether I was going west or east.

'An obviously sinister agitator!' said Jack. 'Accelerate!'

He was pointing to a very old black man in a battered hat. He was sitting on an upturned waste basket outside a store that looked as if it had already been used for riot practice.

We came to an intersection. The road crossed us from north to south (or south to north, depending on which way we were going), but although it seemed about the size of an English motorway, the map had not deigned to mention it.

'We're going wrong!' said Suzan. 'We're going the wrong way! I know it!'

She usually says things like this quite early on in the proceedings. She is usually pretty sceptical about any of us arriving anywhere.

I saw a sign that read SAN BERNARDINO FREEWAY, NORTH.

'We want to go north!' I said.

And before anyone had tried to stop me, I had turned on to the freeway. I am not sure, to be honest, whether it was the San Bernardino Freeway. It might have been the San Diego Freeway. It might have been the San José or the San Andreas Freeway for all I knew or cared. All I knew was it was a freeway headed north.

At least I thought it was going north. It might have been going east or west or south, or straight up in the air, for all I knew. All I did know was that it was taking me away from Airport Boulevard and the sinister cross-section of the local population which had assembled there to warm up for the next bout of disorderly behaviour.

'It's the freeway! Oh my God! It's the freeway!' said Suzan.

She had her head between her knees like someone getting into crash position on an aircraft. I had a lot of sympathy with her. If I had not been sitting behind the wheel I think I would have done the same thing. Nothing in the aircraft, as far as I could remember, had been half as bad as this.

'It's OK!' I yelled. 'We're OK! Is there something on the left?'

There was quite a lot on the left. There was quite a lot on the right, too. Cars, vans, lorries and trucks were coming at us from all directions. All of them, unlike me, seemed to know where they were going. San Bernardino perhaps, or San Diego or San José, or perhaps San Quentin. Perhaps we should go to one of those places. We didn't have to stay in LA. We were on holiday. So far, at any rate, it seemed to hold no attractions for the newcomer whatsoever.

'Keep in!' Suzan was yelling. 'Keep in!'

'Keep in where?' I said.

Unlike an English motorway, where, on the whole, cars overtake only on the right, the custom here seemed to be to drive in whichever bit of the highway you fancied. Sometimes you overtook on the left. Sometimes on the right. Overtaking was rather different than in England. I didn't notice any of the machismo snarls with which English drivers often declare their conquests. No one seemed to be in a particular hurry. They were just all headed to the places where they wanted to go by the route they most favoured, at around 50 or 60 mph. The trouble was, I didn't know where I was going or which, if any, route I favoured. I was, suddenly, a lost 46-year-old Englishman in a hired Ford Aerostar unable to recognize any of the scenes or signs past which he was driving.

Los Angeles seemed to have disappeared. To the right and the left of us were warm hills of pumice-coloured stone and scrub grass and bushes of a green that was a unique blend of the drab and the vivid. I couldn't see any houses.

'Turn off,' yelled Harry, 'turn off now before they get us!'

Ahead was a large sign that said LA CIENEGA BLVD.

'What's a Blvd?' I said.

'It's a boulevard!' said Jack.

Suzan was studying the map. 'We want a boulevard!' she said.

Ned and Jack started to sing their own version of the hit song *Sunset Boulevard*. It bears little relation to Andrew Lloyd-Webber's work of the same name, although at times the tune is eerily similar. It goes –

> Sunset Boulevard
> Up your boulevard
> It's a boulevard
> What a boulevard, etc.

Suzan was yelling at them to stop. I was fighting my way across the six-lane highway to get to the sign that beckoned us towards La Cienega. But when I finally got off the freeway, I was so glad to be in one piece that I allowed the slip road to take me up a hill, round a corner, through a set of lights and then out into a street that was not La Cienega, or indeed any kind of Boulevard.

It looked, I thought, even more like a potential riot zone than Airport Boulevard. A man in a baseball cap who, although not black, seemed ready to commit violence at any moment, was passing us with a large paper bag full of cans. The street looked shabby and worn. At least when I was on the freeway, I knew I was heading north. I was now not sure whether I was headed west, east, north or south. And, as well as not knowing in which direction I was headed, I did not even know the name of the street that was taking me there.

I inched my way down Riot Boulevard, or whatever it was called. I studied the sides of buildings for street signs, but whatever it was called, they had clearly decided to keep its identity secret. It wasn't until Suzan reminded me that the street signs were hung aloft, like christmas decorations, that I looked up to the next sign a block or so away, and read AIRPORT BOULEVARD.

'We're on Airport Boulevard!' I said. 'How did we manage that?'

I turned left at the lights in a desperate attempt to stop the whole cycle beginning again. I had visions of us spending the next few hours driving up the San Bernardino Freeway, turning off for La Cienega, missing the turn-off and driving, once again, down a road that now held me prisoner. It was only after I turned left that I realized that, in America, the street sign hanging above you is the name of the street you're crossing, not the name of the street you're on.

I had brought myself and my family back to where we started, half an hour previously. There ahead of us was the same black woman, walking the same alsatian on the same shabby leather lead. Her shopping bag looked just as heavy, but she was smiling to herself now, as if thinking nothing but peaceful thoughts. I slowed the car, and pulled over to her and said, in a voice that sounded impossibly English –

'Excuse me – we're trying to get to Sunset Boulevard.'

Close to, she did not look at all frightening. She seemed quite the reverse. She gave me a broad grin.

'Where you're from?' she said.

'London, England,' I said.

The woman smiled. 'You're a long way from home,' she said.

She pointed up ahead. 'Take a left three blocks down,' she said, 'head up on La Cienega until you hit Sunset. Where you headed?'

'Hollywood.'

'Take a left on Sunset.'

She looked in at the five of us. We grinned out in placatory, English fashion. Her grin just kept on and on. Her hands, I could see, were scarred with work. There was dirt under the finger nails.

'I seen you earlier,' she said. 'I thought you was maybe Welsh. You Welsh?'

I was grinning now.

'I'm a bit Welsh,' I said. 'My father was Welsh.'

She shook her head in wonder at this remark. Then she said – 'You ain't Welsh. You Australian!'

She stood watching as, still laughing, I drove the Ford Aerostar up towards La Cienega. I watched her, too, in the driving mirror. Harry turned to her just before I headed north and waved. She waved back. She was my fourth real American. After her, we met more and more – and some of them weren't faces any more, just glimpsed expressions or hands taking dollars at a check-out counter. But I still remember her. I still think of her and her alsatian walking along a shabby street in downtown LA.

21

3

Hollywood

The Chateau Marmont hotel in West Hollywood is where the actor John Belushi died. There are, apparently, tours organized to the room where it happened. I have the idea that he committed suicide, although why he should have done so I do not know. Perhaps he waited too long for room service.

There were times when I contemplated suicide at the Chateau Marmont – most notably when I was presented with the bill. It is a gloomy, rather sinister establishment. The waiters seem to have been carried up from some dark, underground place, and when they tell you to have a nice day or inform you you're welcome to thank them, they do not sound as if their hearts are in it. There is a curiously English quality about them.

But on the first evening we spent there I was American enough for the entire staff. I had, now I begin to think of it, been getting more and more American as we moved from plane to Baggage Retrieval to Airport Boulevard and along to La Cienega. By the time we hit Sunset, I was auditioning heavily for the role of native Angelino.

'I'll call Gavin!' I said, as soon as we checked into our room. 'I'll make a meeting with him!' It was now about half past seven.

Suzan pointed out that I had by now been awake for nearly twenty-one hours. I was in no condition to walk up a flight of stairs, let alone 'make a meeting'. There was something about the way she said this which I did not like.

'I have to make meetings while we're here!' I said. 'I have to get an LA agent.'

There have been times over the last twenty years when I have imagined that one day I will be paid $300,000 for writing heart-warming rubbish. There comes a time in every writer's life when he feels he is owed $300,000 for writing heart-warming rubbish.

'I am writing a movie,' said a writer friend of mine, shortly before I left for America. Before I had time to ask what it was, he added: '$300,000.' I didn't really need to ask what it was about after that. It could have been a musical about a man who turned into a skunk or a comedy set in ancient Egypt.

You never hear what happens to these movies. People just back you up against a wall at parties and torment you with the amount they are being paid for them. But the same people do not come up to you at other parties and tell you how Ted Lewenstein on the coast told them that the second draft sucked.

I have written one film for a major Hollywood motion picture company. I was not given a swimming pool while I was writing it. In fact I was given just about enough money for the tube fare between Wimbledon and Wardour Street, where the film company's offices were located. At one point, one of the executives said to me –

'They love your movie on the coast!'

'They love my movie on the coast!' I assumed that, very soon, an air ticket, a limousine and possibly an attractive female vice-president would be on their way to SW15. I waited a week, I waited two weeks, I waited three weeks. The next time I tried the head office of the company, a different man answered the phone. He did not love my movie on the coast. He did not love anything about me or my movie on the coast. When I asked someone who he was, they replied, 'Oh, he's Ralph Sternstein's cousin. That's all he is.' I think they must have fired the man who loved my movie on the coast. I think probably all the people who loved my movie on the coast were hurried, quietly, from the luxurious offices off Wilshire Boulevard. They were probably all told never to darken the doors of the motion picture company ever again.

But in spite of that experience I still dream of earning huge amounts of money for a manuscript *that has a maximum length of 120 pages.* In fact, if a Hollywood movie is more than 120 pages long they start to get very worried indeed.

'What's it like?' they say on the coast.

'Well, it's 125 pages!' say the agents in London, New York or Paris, and hear at the other end of the phone thousands of miles away a sharp intake of breath. It's 125 pages and he wants $300,000! Come on! It's got to be a 120-page movie if you want that kind of money. It's got to be expensive, sure, but it's also got to be *the right length*.

As to what it's all about, well fuck what it's all about. It could be about midgets in space or X in the old west or adultery in Switzerland. So long as it's got Bruce Willis in it, it'll be fine.

I looked out of the window of our room at Sunset Boulevard. It was possible that Bruce Willis was out there somewhere. He might even be that figure on the other side of the street, trudging his way towards the Virgin Megastore. Jack had informed me earlier that there were more compact discs there than in the whole of the United Kingdom.

Bruce Willis didn't walk though, did he? He had enough money never to have to walk again. But he was out there. Harrison Ford and Steven Spielberg, Julia Roberts and Whoopi Goldberg and Richard Gere and George Lucas – they were all out there. All I had to do was to get out there amongst them and wave a copy of one of the four-part TV series that had received such favourable previews in the London Evening Standard, all those years ago.

They would only be able to say no. I was here. I was vital. I was full of ideas. I was a salesman. I was determined to get my foot in the door. I was American.

Suzan pointed out that I wasn't American. I was simply an Englishman who had been awake for nearly twenty-four hours.

'Ring him in the morning,' she said.

'This *is* the morning!' I said. 'To me it is the morning!'

And with these words I followed her to bed. It had got dark while I was thinking about Bruce Willis. Somewhere along the way I had eaten a Caesar salad and drunk two beers, a bourbon whisky and a bottle of Chardonnay. The Chardonnay, the beer, the bourbon and the Caesar salad had now joined the three in-flight meals, the two airport-size bottles of red wine, the half-bottle of champagne, the four cups of coffee and the three bottles of Evian water that I had eaten and drunk since leaving England. I was now no longer sure in what order I had eaten or drunk any of them. There were moments when I thought I must have gobbled the whole lot down in one ghastly, orgiastic moment, just after I had driven along Airport Boulevard and seen a female rioter who wasn't a female rioter but, suddenly, a Hertz hire-car official saying, in what sounded like a New York accent, 'Limtedlibilladywaiver?' And I was saying, 'I want it. Whatever it is. I want it.' Whether it's Bruce Willis or Whoopi Goldberg or the Virgin Megastore or San Bernardino or a contract for $300,000, I want it. I'm an Amurkan. I want it. I want it now.

I was asleep.

At least I thought I was asleep. I was too jet-lagged to know if I was asleep or awake. All I did know was that, whether I was asleep or awake or in a weird combination of the two, I was in America, and the next time I woke up I would still be in America. There would be hundreds more Americans out there to phone and meet and hire cars from and ask directions of and, asleep or awake, I was going to go right ahead and get just about as much of them as I could.

When I awoke somebody was shouting in my ear. It was Ned.

'We're going,' he said, 'to Universal Studios! Up you get!'

Ned is seventeen. I look at him once or twice a week and find it hard to recall that he was once not much larger than a chicken. And almost as hard to understand. He is a tall, pale-faced youth, whose hair falls evenly about his face giving him the air of one of those anonymous young people of Sienna or Florence whose faces stare out at us from the Renaissance paintings in the Uffizi.

'I have to phone Gavin!' I said.

'Shut up!' said Suzan. 'We must go to Universal Studios.'

Perhaps my family were all trying to sell film scripts. Perhaps they had all arranged meetings. Perhaps they had all got contracts. They stood, I told myself, about as much chance as I did. At least they weren't forty-six-year-old white males from Wimbledon.

'I want to go on the *Back to the Future* ride!' said Harry. 'Akhatar says its brilliant!'

Akhatar has been on the *Back to the Future* ride. Akhatar has been all over Universal Studios. So have Fromayne, the Barraclough twins, Puller and Jemashe, the Eastons and Heineken's younger brother. The whole of the lower school of King's College, Wimbledon seem already to have experienced what I was about to undergo.

Shouldn't I have done all this years ago? Why was all of this so strange to me, so late in my life? Why did the trip to Universal Studios feel like the crossing of a frontier, when in fact the journey is a completely mundane one? To be fair, a part of me was as excited as Harry, Akhatar or the Barraclough twins or any other member of King's College Junior School might have been, catching sight of these things for the first time. I felt as much in awe as when I first saw Notre-Dame or bounced out of Beersheba in an Israeli army lorry and looked out over the Negev desert. There was nothing obviously strange about my surroundings. And yet there was. As we went down to the van, and as I pulled out on to Sunset Boulevard, there were moments when I thought I was passing through an England reworked by a giant, wayward child. If you took the corner of a shopping mall in the south of London where I live, did it up to five times the size, did the same with a garage (I nearly said, wanted to say, so seductive was this place, *gas station*), and then placed them like child's toys at either end of a gigantic plaza garnished with palm trees under an infinitely pale blue sky, you might start to get an idea of the landscape I had wandered into. It wasn't so much a landscape as a piece of a gigantic board game. I seemed to be driving down a road the size of an English motorway decorated with Chevvy pick-ups and big alien Fords at unreal intervals along its surface, and this was only a boulevard, for Christ's sake! This was a Blvd! To the Americans driving past me in the ghostly ordered way in which good Americans drive, this was just an ordinary road. From here we were going on to an even bigger road, and we were going to drive along that road, too! As had Akhatar, the Barraclough twins and half the population of

King's Wimbledon! And, if they were right, it was going to be the biggest and best of all the fun palaces in the world.

I have been to a few fun palaces in my time. I have queued for forty-five minutes for the water slide at Chessington World of Adventure. I have taken my children on the flumes at Thorpe Park. I once put my back out rather badly on the dodgems at Putney fair.

But none of these things had prepared for me the approach to Universal Studios.

It was almost inconceivable that something on this scale could be devoted solely to entertainment. I spent some minutes looking up at a structure that was about the size of the front door of Rheims Cathedral. It was some time before I realized it was the entrance. Behind it was a gigantic gateway, arched like a viaduct and easily wide enough to accommodate a small train. The bright primary colours, the sun that had only just cleared the mountains over to the east, the miles of clear concrete to the distant twinkling hangers of the studio lot conspired to suggest that what waited for us on the other side was something as uncomplicated as Paradise.

Over to our left a group of fat people in shorts were eating hamburgers and drinking coke. Over to our right a group of twenty or thirty elderly Dutch persons were getting out of a large coach. Ahead of us waiting for the pleasure park to open (it was still barely seven o'clock in the morning) were some thirty or forty Hispanic men, women and children, who all seemed to be related to each other. There was a tremendous air of anticipation about the place.

'First,' said Harry, 'I'm going on the *Back to the Future* ride.'

He was wearing a blue New York Knicks baseball cap, a red Phoenix Suns T-shirt and a pair of bright yellow shorts. He looked, I thought, fairly spectacular. His face was luminous with excitement.

I followed him as the gates opened and the first visitors hurried through. All of us, I noticed, were half running, half walking, like people on their way to the site of a miracle. But Harry was well ahead of us.

'He could be an American, couldn't he?' said Suzan.

'He bloody is an American,' said Ned grimly.

'I think,' said Jack, in the slow, considered way he has, 'he wants to be an American. But he's not quite one yet.'

Harry turned to us. His wide face split into a grin. He made an extravagant gesture, slapped his thigh and set off for the *Back to the Future* ride at a slow run.

'What is he?' said Ned.

Jack thought for a moment.

'He is ludicrous,' he said, 'basically.'

American culture has conquered the world by the simple expedient of assuming that it has already done so. Americans do not feel the need to explain themselves and, in one sense, they require no explanation. This, of course, is the one thing about them that it is quite impossible to explain.

Americans know, for example, that everyone likes Coca-Cola and everyone likes hamburgers. Because they do. Americans know that everyone likes the Universal Studios tour. Because they do. Americans know too that if you go on the Universal Studios tour you will *know* that *Back to the Future* is a film directed by Robert Zemeckis in which a loony old scientist takes Michael J Fox off on a ride to the future. They know that you know that *Back Draft* is a film about fire-fighting, and that the shark in *Jaws* is the most famous fish in the world. They know this to be the case. And, hard though it is to admit it, you also know that it is true. Otherwise – why are you there?

Forget the Parthenon or the sonnets of Shakespeare, I muttered to myself, grimly, my love affair with America taking a sour turn as I traipsed after my youngest son, these are the real cultural reference points of our world – the awful, undisputable tautology that says that Mickey Mouse is Mickey Mouse is Mickey Mouse.

The *Back to the Future* ride involved being strapped into a small car in a dark room while a subjective camera swoops down valleys into volcanos and swerves, unbraked, towards the mouths of dinosaurs. The car you are in sways in time to the movie. It seems to throw you into the image. You are entirely at its service. If you can forget – as everyone else in my family did – that you are watching a film, then you will walk through distant galaxies, skim the surface of ancient ruins and rise up into the jaws of monsters until you find yourself screaming out loud in fear. But, if a voice inside you says, 'This is another of their damn movies!' (and a voice inside me started to do just that), oh, then as the car bucks and moves underneath you, rather than ecstasy you will experience motion sickness.

It was in the *Back to the Future* ride that I began to suspect that in America there might be another country – a frightening, nausea-inspiring monster that made nothing out of something and something out of nothing. It was in the *Back to the Future* ride that, as Suzan, Ned, Jack and Harry howled with real or simulated fear and cheered each new celluloid surprise – I started to feel sick.

I didn't stop feeling sick after the thing stopped.

I felt sick as we staggered out into the light. I felt sick as we went down an escalator that advertised itself as the second longest in the world. I felt sick as Harry, snapping his fingers like a Spanish dancer, ordered popcorn, more Coke, extra burgers with cheese and many other things that no sane person should be eating at seven-thirty in the morning. I felt sick most of all when the four of them hurried off to something called the ET ride.

'What is it?' I called out after them, unable to move from the bench where I was sitting.

'You sit on a bicycle and they throw you off a cliff!' said Ned, cackling. Jack cackled too. I sat there in the Californian sunshine. The earth moved for me and my stomach moved with it. I put my head in my hands.

'Walker!' said a large black man to his son. 'Stop doing that running away shit! You did that at Niagara Falls!'

I put my head in my hands between my knees. I was starting to feel very strange indeed. If I carried on like this for much longer people would soon be queuing to see me.

When a poor man eats a chicken, says the Yiddish proverb, *one of them is sick*. Either I, or Universal Studios in Hollywood, was sick. For a brief moment I thought I might not be at fault, but when I saw my family return ('Hey, there's Nige! There's poor old dad, how *are* you?') I realized that for the moment it wasn't America but Nigel Williams that was out of step with how things ought to be.

They swept past me towards a line of tram cars and I followed. Each tram car was full of clean, optimistic Americans mixed in with slightly less clean and slightly less optimistic Europeans. In the driver's car was another confident, assertive young man with a moustache who seemed ecstatically happy to be driving about 200 tourists to a studio lot he had, presumably, seen several hundred thousand times before.

'Ahead of us,' he called, 'is the Bates Motel. The motel actually used in the film *Psycho*, up there on the hill. Note the clever way the house has been designed. It's smaller than it looks in the movie but was always shot from below to make it look more sinister and brooding!'

We saw flash floods and subway disasters and cowboy towns and Italian villages, and the New York of the 1920s where tall department stores, bars, hotels, fire stations and offices all stood stiffly at attention, none of them more than a few inches thick, all of them made out of plywood. We saw the shark from *Jaws*, the subway crash from *Beverly Hills Cop III*, we saw burnt out jeeps, buildings that could be blown up to order, and we saw the house where Cary Grant proposed to Doris Day, and the house next door where Scarlet O'Hara said she didn't give a damn. We saw the house where Tom Hanks shrunk into a twelve-year-old boy, and round the corner I think we might have seen a path that shook to the giant dinosaurs of *Jurassic Park*.

At least, I think we saw those things. I can't remember, now, what we saw there, and what I saw in darkened cinemas in Kilburn, Finchley, Putney and Bayswater. There is no country in the world to have invested so heavily in fantasy as America. Its dreams – like everyone's – are incredibly expensive and almost impossibly hard to maintain. But when solidified as they have been in the sun-drenched acres of Hollywood or Florida, they have a habit of shaming European ambitions. American art is a unique reflection of the aspirations of its people – that is its blessing and its curse. As I rocketed back to base round the curve of a hill, I thought how impossible such a place would be back home, where cathedrals are no longer vulgar, and our own great pleasure palaces, from Euro-Disney to the Roman forum, are crumbling.

I tried to picture an English voice saying – 'This is the actual field where Kenneth Williams kissed the matron's bum in *Carry on Doctor* ... Over there is the mountain where Jean Gabin very nearly gave up in *La Grande Illusion*.' No. The influential American philosophers are lawyers, scientists or idiots. And it is the idiots – from Thoreau to Disney – who have had the most commanding influence on the culture.

'This,' said Harry, 'is great!'

'It is,' I said, in the most sincere voice I could manage. 'It's great!' I caught Jack looking at me sharply. He swept back his dirty blond hair with the elegant fingers of his right hand. He had, as so often, the dangerous watchfulness I associate with the larger primates. He gave the impression that he was thinking interesting things to which no one else in the family had access.

We were back at base. After the tour there was the animal show, and after the animal show there was the Flintstones, and after the Flintstones there was (mercifully) the exit.

'I'm going to phone Gavin,' I said. 'I need an LA agent.'

'I don't see why Gavin should get you an LA agent!' said Suzan.

I looked across the valley at the hills. They seemed the same as they had been when we went in. But the signs of life down there had a strange look. Was it the dry mountain landscape that gave things that unfinished look? Or was it that, if there was life here, it had been upstaged by the entertainers? I could make out a highway. There were buildings too – a large aluminium square that looked as if it might have been a factory of some kind. Beyond that, two or three huge steel sheds squatted awkwardly among the browns and greens of the hillside. There were people in this town. In order to understand the place I had better go and meet some of them.

'We'll go and see Gavin,' I said, as we went towards the car. 'I need to meet real Americans.'

Suzan gave me a curious look.

'Gavin,' she said, 'is an Englishman. Isn't he?'

4

All I want is a swimming pool

Gavin went to Hollywood about ten years ago.

At first, people in London were not impressed.

'Gavin', I heard them say at parties, 'has gone to Hollywood! What a waste!'

I think I imagined, at first, that he would soon be back. When he showed no signs of returning, I scanned the credits of imported American films to see if I could see his name. When his credit finally did appear, it was on a work of such banality that I couldn't possibly connect it with the sensitive soul I had known in SW15.

'He'll be back soon,' I said, 'he can't *seriously* be happy making films like that. Where is the wit, the sensitivity, the intellectual rigour and the passion of that wonderful half-hour play he did for the BBC in 1981?'

I did not of course mention that the play had been written by me.

And then I happened to glance at *Variety* in someone's office, and noticed that the film on which Gavin's name had appeared had grossed hundreds of millions of dollars. It had been shown in Austria, Hong Kong, France, Indonesia, Russia, Malaysia, China, Finland, Norway, and almost everywhere in the world apart from Iceland. It had even made its way to Wimbledon.

'Gavin', I said to people, 'has sold out.'

A couple of years passed. I was emboldened to hope that the man had had the decency to have some kind of permanent breakdown. He was perhaps, I decided, an alcoholic or in the throws of some unhappy love affair, preferably with someone of the same sex. Perhaps, I told myself, he had made a follow-up and the studio had decided not to release it.

Imagine my surprise one afternoon when I took my family to UCI Whiteleys and, as I was settling into my seat, the first thing I saw on the screen were the words:

A GAVIN SIMPSON FILM

Gavin Simpson is not, as you may have guessed, the man's real name. I do not wish to give him any more publicity than he has already received.

I knew from that first moment that there was something wrong with the piece. Those four words had sharpened my critical faculties to a Leavisite pitch.

It was a 'comedy'. A comedy of such crudity that I could scarcely believe anyone apart from Simpson's immediate family would be prepared to watch it for longer than ten minutes. There were cute kids and wacky grannies and kind moms and dads, and somehow or other, towards the end, there was Christmas. As I shifted further down in my seat, I squinted along the row. My family and I would soon rise from our seats and slip out into the street below. We would soon have forgotten all about this 'Gavin Simpson' film. To my surprise I saw that they were laughing. They were squirming around in their seats and stuffing handkerchiefs in their mouths. Jack was slapping his thighs and calling for more. Suzan's shoulders were shaking with laughter. As presumably, in the weeks to come, shoulders would be shaking from Botany Bay to the Straits of Gibraltar.

Over the next few years there were more films *de* Gavin Simpson, and each one seemed to gross more than the one that had preceded it. The man, it seemed, could do no wrong. Presumably, by now, the studios were falling over each other to offer millions of dollars simply for the privilege of being in the same room as him. I was amazed, I told myself as we drove down Sunset Boulevard to our next port of call – the John Paul Getty museum – that I had not in the months that followed ripped his name out of my address book. But there was still some fight left in me. As I dialled his number from a payphone in the museum, I cast around for a suitable opening line.

'Are you still in films?', or 'Are we ever going to win you back for art, Gavin?'

It was important not to let the man know he was getting to me.

The young man who answered the phone said –

'Gavin Simpson Incorporated.' I'm not entirely sure that that is what he said. It might have been 'Gavin Simpson Limited.' or 'Gavin Simpson Conglomerates.' or 'Gavin Simpson plc'. But whatever it was it suggested that Gavin Simpson was about as well known over here as Colonel Sanders.

'Is um ... er ... Gavin Simpson there?' I said.

'Gavin is out at the moment,' said the young man, 'but this is his assistant speaking. May I help?'

This was a bit more like it. Presumably Gavin Simpson Incorporated was not a five-storey building with its own parking lot and Gavin Simpson's name all over the front in letters sixteen feet high. It was presumably one room and a fridge in North Hollywood. Simpson was probably in the same room as his assistant, signalling at him wildly. He probably assumed I was one of his many creditors.

'It's an old friend of his here,' I said, 'from England.'

When we got back to the Chateau Marmont that evening there was a message from Gavin. He would be delighted to see us, he said, for brunch the next day.

'Come up,' the message ran, 'and bring your trunks.' Harry said he thought this was an odd thing to say.

'Are we going to the Leisure Centre?' he said.

I said through clenched teeth that Gavin Simpson probably had his own swimming pool. Harry seemed impressed by this. I said it was nothing much. There was a man in Barnes, I said, who had his own swimming pool. If he was so desperate about it, we could have our own swimming pool. Suzan gave a kind of snort.

'Yes,' she said, 'if you want to get back that small, inflatable one I lent to Marjorie Parsons!'

When we drove up there next morning, there was quite a lot of discussion about the pool. Harry wanted to know if there would be a jacuzzi. 'Of course there'll be a jacuzzi,' said Jack in terms of great contempt, 'there are *always* jacuzzis.'

Suzan, who had not brought her swimming trunks, said that there were also liable to be a lot of thin, young, brown women. Ned asked what was wrong with thin, young, brown, women. They were, he said, in short supply in Wimbledon.

Gavin's house is somewhere in the Hollywood hills. I'm not going to say where in case you all hot-foot up there next time you're in Los Angeles and bang on his front door claiming to be a friend of mine. The first thing I saw as I turned into his drive, which runs off a narrow road on the crest of a hill, was a small blue sign on which I could just about read the words:

ARMED RESPONSE

I braked hard and read the small print. It seemed to suggest that there were people in the bushes with orders to shoot anyone without an appointment. I asked myself about the status of the message Gavin had left for us at our hotel. How seriously was I expected? And what kind of armed response might one expect if I wasn't? Were we talking small arms? Sniper fire? Or was there the odd Vietnam Vet with a bazooka crouching up there in the stony ground under the twisted trees?

'They probably only shoot at your legs,' said Ned.

I said we should probably pin a white flag to the front of the car. Suzan started to mutter darkly about what she would do to anyone who tried to shoot at her. Her hair was well down over her eyes, and her shoulders were at a no-nonsense angle. I inched the Aerostar down a steep track that led away from the road to a grove of small trees, and out on to the hillside.

I had not realized how far up the mountain we had come. We were looking south across Los Angeles. In the distance were a group of huge skyscrapers that, in the brilliant sunshine, had taken on the blue of the sky. Immediately in front of us, carved into a near-vertical section of the hillside, was what must have been Gavin Simpson's house.

I thought at first it was a fairly modest affair. The house front, a broad oak door, a low roof, and to its left a set of fake gothic windows set into a solid, antique wooden frame, seemed to be a bid for the Spanish colonial. But as the road took us down the mountain, below the level of the frontage, we saw that behind it, jutting out from the bare rock, was a confection in wood and glass and steel that had the air of an ambitious greenhouse. Beyond that was a gigantic verandah supported on huge steel columns which went down into the hill below it, and to the left of the verandah was another Spanish colonial effort that was about the size of my house in London. This presumably was where Gavin Simpson kept his dog or visiting Englishmen.

On the verandah were quite a lot of thin, young, brown women. There was a man in a white jacket handing round a tray of drinks, and two or three young men, one of whom was in trunks. As I got out from the car one of them leapt into the air, positioned himself gracefully, upside down about six feet from the ground, and disappeared head-first into the unseen surface below. There was a thud, a splash, and even at this distance (or was it my imagination?) a distant tang of chlorine.

'They have got a pool!' said Harry, his eyes wide. 'They really have!'

'They're an awful lot of work!' I said, as the five of us struggled up towards the front door. 'An awful lot of work.'

We were just at the front door when a well-built, middle-aged man who looked as if he had spent the last ten years playing tennis in the open air stepped out and threw both his hands in the air.

'Nigel!' he said.

Fearing he was about to embrace me, I took a pace backwards. He continued forwards. His face was vaguely familiar, but his voice was not. He was not obviously English, but neither would I have said he was American. I waited for him to say something else so that I could start to pin him down to a particular section of the globe.

'It's fanterstic ta say you!' he went on. Was he Scottish? Or Chinese? There was something completely unnerving about his vowels. Was he, perhaps, not from this earth at all?

'Sich a graet thung!' he was saying. 'It's bin yars!'

The drama of each word was almost unbearable. He would

start out with Transatlantic dashed with Euro, mutate suddenly into a brief flash of English gentleman, and then come up with a fog-horn-like noise that sounded as if all his vocal cords were being squeezed through a mangle. The facial expressions that went with this – shubunkin-like movement of the lips, an Al Jolson rolling of the eyes, and the arm movements of a Mexican street trader – suggested that his basal ganglia had been removed and he was now operated like a string puppet by someone high up in Paramount Pictures.

For this – unbelievable as it seemed – was Gavin Simpson.

'Coem threw!' he was saying. 'Wear owl out b'th pule!'

He still had the look of a man trying to embrace me. His arms were still up in the air. Short of chasing me around the grounds, I had decided, he was not going to get his hands on any part of my anatomy. My body at least was still my own.

We walked through several cool, spacious rooms. There was a copy of Knut Hamsun's *Hunger* on one of the sofas, and next to that a collected edition of the poetry of A E Housman. Maybe the next film on his agenda was '*A Shropshire Lad*. A Gavin Simpson Film with Housman's mother played by Demi Moore'.

On a huge iron table by a casement window overlooking the garden was a gigantic spread of bagels, smoked salmon, cream cheese, orange juice, coffee and champagne. Suzan moved ahead of us. A faraway look came into Ned's eyes as he looked out on to the verandah. Harry's face, too; his cheeks, eyes and mouth were individually and collectively becoming more and more circular.

'She's got no bra on!' he whispered. One of the young, thin, brown women was in the state he described.

I gulped, coughed and began to make brisk conversation with Simpson. I did not ask him why he was talking like a duck or whether he had rented this house or these people for the day simply in order to humiliate me. I found myself saying –

'Great to see you!'

'Grrat t'see yew!' he said. 'Wanner swam?'

'Sure,' I said. 'Lass swam!'

'Yeah!' said Harry. 'Lass swam!'

And pulling off his clothes he ran towards the swimming pool, and the young, thin, brown woman smiled at him and he smiled back.

Gavin took the rest of us (Ned, after a few careful glances in the direction of the young, thin, brown women, had decided to swim later) to the edge of the verandah.

'The guys hew bilt thiz, right?' he said, 'worked fer aboet a duller a dae. Whach is wat is so incredibble oebaat Amurka. It's glory or grovel!'

He told us how the workers had had to dig the foundations of the house by hand, since the hillside was too steep to get excavating equipment in place. They were all Hispanic, he said, probably illegal immigrants. They worked from eight in the morning until ten at night, for hardly any money.

'It's like the Pharaohs!' he said, lapsing suddenly into English. 'It's like ancient Egypt!'

We looked across at South Central. When the riots had happened, he said, all the neighbourhood houses lived in by agents, stars, directors, and sometimes even writers, had got together and formed a posse. They had barricaded the road that led down from the hillside into the rest of town. They were all armed, he said, and prepared to fight for what was theirs.

'Well,' I said, 'I think I would fight to defend this.'

'Knarr!' said Simpson, 'and to think it waz arl paed for by … ' Here he mentioned the name of one of his films. I hoped he wasn't going to ask me what I thought of it, but it had been very clear very quickly that one Englishman's opinion of a film that had wacky grannies, cute kids, caring moms and dads, and of course Christmas, would be irrelevant. What was one voice among so many?

And sitting with him by the pool, I found myself wondering whether my convictions about culture, made up as they are of too much bitterness and too much reading, really did matter. I like *you*, says the cured homosexual in William Burroughs's book, and *I like apple pie*. That is the American equation. It lulls your senses to sleep. It calls, silent like, to your twisted English soul and says *relax, don't fight it, relax …*

We were drinking and eating and talking. Ned, who had got into his swimming trunks, was lying face down talking to one of the young, thin, brown women. An American with a beard, who turned out to be a screen-writer, was telling us how he found England cold and unfriendly. And we were telling him that we found Americans warm and helpful and direct and honest and open. And we believed it, for in the sunshine and the champagne, the country seemed all-of-a-sudden anxious to please again.

'You can bring my breakfast to me!' called Harry. 'I'm in the jacuzzi.'

I was to learn that America does that. It's like an unpredictable guest. One minute you have your arms around each other like old friends, and the next you're banged up with a screaming madman who seems to be trying to kill you for no particular reason.

'When you see Ernglish pibble orff the plane at LAX, they bob out like that y'kno, saying I've been a gud buoy, c'n I have my pension naow. You think its incradibbly smorl and dull and –'

I laughed. England was incredibly small and dull. It was probably, if you like, incredibly smorl and daell. Later he took us to see Rick and Jane, who lived on Coldwater Canyon. Their house had its own recording studio, and the pool had underwater windows so that the porn king who had owned it before them could watch naked ladies swimming past while he sipped his after-dinner brandy. Harry had his tea in their jacuzzi. Gavin and Rick and Jane talked about projects. At any moment, I found myself thinking, Marlon Brando might be dropping in. Then someone said he actually lived next door. Afterwards we all went off down towards the coast to see an English actor, where we drank Californian white wine and looked across from his pool at the ocean. Harry had his dinner in his jacuzzi. He said the actor had the best jacuzzi. I said it wasn't the most expensive jacuzzi. Harry said that money wasn't everything. By this time I was rather drunk. I put my arms around Gavin Simpson, and the two of us looked out at the Pacific.

'Do you miss England?' I said. Simpson looked across at Rick and Jane and the American screen-writer and the English actor. Then he looked at Suzan and Ned and Jack and Harry. Ned was talking to one of the young, thin, brown women in Italian. Jack was reading David Copperfield on a lilo in the pool.

'Not really,' he said.

'No,' I said. 'Neither do I.'

He pointed out that I had only been away from the country for two days. I found this an astonishingly witty remark.

'Seriously,' I said, 'I could live here.'

Gavin Simpson folded his muscular arms. He put his head to one side and looked at me quizzically. Then he smiled, his teeth as big and white and strong as everything else about him. He took in my Marks & Spencer shorts, grubby with travel, my Millets hiking boots, my dirty T-shirt and my shabby uncombed hair. When he spoke he was the London boy I had known ten years ago – to the life.

'I don't think so,' he said; 'not really.'

5

Reservations about Indians

About six months prior to our departure, Suzan had started rat-tling on about some people called the Hopi Indians. She seemed somewhat vague about what they looked like or where they lived, but the little she did know about them had obviously inspired her to find out more. I could not, for some reason, get her off the subject. At first it was preferable to some of her other subjects – my habit of leaving my socks in the hall, for example, or the question of whose turn it might be to take the children to school – but after a week or so of her banging on about them, I'd rather taken against the Hopi Indians.

The guidebook she consulted hinted that they might be equal-ly unkeen on me. If you wanted to see them, the guidebook said, you were advised to book well in advance. You were liable to be told that they did not wish to see anybody.

'They live in mesas,' Suzan said, 'thousands of years old. They have their own culture.'

They did sound, at least, like a refreshing change from Gavin Simpson. There were other Indians out there as well, she said. The Hopi lived in the middle of something called the Navajo reservation. This area, she said, belonged completely and utterly to the Navajo. Ever since a treaty made with the US government in 1868, it had been 100 per cent Navajo.

'I bet', I said, 'that it isn't really Navajo. I read *Bury My Heart at Wounded Knee*. I know what the Americans did to the Indians. They'll all be in blankets, drunk, rolling around on the ground covered in fleas.'

She said that were that to be the case I would be likely to fit in well. The Navajo, she said, weren't like that at all. In fact, she said, the Navajo would make me look pretty primitive.

She added that that would not be difficult.

I had booked us rooms at a Holiday Inn in Chinle, Arizona, and two days after we had dined with Gavin Simpson we took Highway 15 east out of LA.

This sounds deceptively simple. What we actually did was to scream at each other for about half an hour while we drove around Los Angeles looking for the way out. Then, when we found a freeway, Suzan crouched underneath the dashboard until we got to San Bernardino. Even when in the safety position, she flinched every time she heard a car pass us. The city was making me nervous again, too. Just as if it had never really started, so it seemed unable to finish. As we ran out east there were always suburban strips on the other side of the trees, fringing the highway, and seemingly endless turn-offs to ACACIA DRV or WESTERN BLVD. We were only just clearing the city when we saw the sign to Highway 15 which runs up to Las Vegas. We were to take it as far as Highway 40 which runs from Barstow at the south extreme of the Mojave desert on into North Carolina. There was a petrol station there, where a big, rumpled man said to me, 'You need gas – just look for those big, orange circles in the sky.' When we climbed out of the air-conditioned car, the wind coming off the desert felt as if someone was holding a hairdryer to your face. Above us to our left was the San Antonio mountain and the dirty white and bleached greens of the Mojave.

When we got back into the car, everyone seemed calmer. Jack was reading David Copperfield. Ned was owled over an edition of the poems of Wilfred Owen. Harry was listening to the recorded adventures of Sherlock Holmes. Suzan sat in the seat next to me, eyes wide with wonder, as we pulled up towards Barstow. Beyond Barstow were straight roads to arid, empty ground. Where a town appeared, it was difficult to see what it was there for. The names hinted at the arbitrary nature of the settlements: Needles, Yucca, Kingman – and on up to Searchlight and Boulder City. There was no history or sentiment in them. They were the casual bequests of people who had been through here long ago and passed on to other things.

The desert, the highway, the stunted shrubs, and the occasional bungalow abandoned in a waste of powdery ground with only a barbed-wire fence to keep off the wilderness, all seemed as if they were waiting for something. The huge trucks, with their vertical exhausts poking up by the bonnet like a Crusader's lance and their snub, squat noses that gave them the look of ugly, angry dogs, thundered towards us from the east and bore down on us from the west. They, not we, seemed natural in the landscape. Everything human is negated in the desert. The car, too, helped to make what was on the other side of the windows unreal. Half frozen by the air conditioning, we rolled up towards Arizona, and the only things marking the passage of our journey were the emptying and filling of the petrol tank, and the radio stations that seemed to change every fifty or sixty miles. On one of them the only entertainment offered was a man reading from and discussing the Book of Genesis. On another I heard country music that would have sounded unsophisticated in Nashville. We drove east without stopping, and it was dark when we pulled into the Little America motel, Flagstaff, Arizona. The trip had taken us nine hours. The man in the restaurant said –

'Hello, I am Gary and I am your server tonight.'

'Hello,' said Harry, 'I am Harry and I would like a lemonade!'

Gary did not seem bothered by this. I noticed throughout our trip that most Americans found Harry's behaviour completely normal. Gary asked us where we were from and where we were going, and how we found it, and we said that we were from England, and we were going to the Navajo reservation, and we found it fine, and he said good, that was fine. Then we ate steaks, drank white California wine and went back to the motel room, where Harry said –

'Are these Indians … you know … tame? Or are they sort of … running around?'

'I think,' I said in the darkness, 'they are running around. But to be honest I am not quite sure what they are really doing. Ask your mother.'

Suzan said that she didn't know what they were doing either.

That was why we were going to see them. One of the things they were probably doing right know, she added, was going to sleep. She advised us to do the same.

I lay awake for some time, thinking about Indians.

My mental picture of an Indian reservation was not unlike a concentration camp. I saw it as fairly small with a lot of high wire fencing around it. Inside the fencing were Indians. They were looking out at the landscape as wistfully as a dog in a kennel. Outside were Americans taking photographs of them with the unjustified superiority of visitors to a zoo.

Looking at the map it was fairly easy to see that the Navajo reservation was not going to be anything much like this. It seemed to be about 25,000 miles square, stretching from the Grand Canyon in the west over to New Mexico and the Colorado border in the east. South it stretched down all the way to Highway 40, and north it reached up to the shore of Lake Powell and the border with Utah. If it was any kind of zoo, it was one of those wildlife parks where you drove around and glimpsed the animals through binoculars.

When I said this to Suzan the next morning, she said I was being tasteless. The Navajo reservation was, she said, a victory for the Indian nation as a whole.

'The Navajo nation,' she said, reading from a guidebook, 'is a prosperous and hard-working group of Native Americans. They were turned off their land in the 1860s to a place called Bosque Redondo where a huge number of them died. But thanks to a treaty made in 1868 with the US government they are now a completely *independent* state within America. They farm and dig for minerals and run a prosperous tourist industry. They make rugs and jewellery and ...' I said I thought they sounded depressingly like Americans. I said I thought Indians ought to be wild and free and riding round on horses and shooting at white men. It was what they did best, I said. Suzan said I was being silly.

It was not long after dawn next morning when we drove up to the Painted Desert where the ruins of calcified trees lie in the midst of rocks that seemed to have only just stopped moving.

They grew pink in the rising sun, and in the valleys, weird shapes grew out of the shadows. The guide book said they were solidified mineral deposits – silicon, copper, iron oxide, manganese and carbon. But at first I thought they were the outrageously pretty pinks and reds of a pastel drawing. And then, on closer inspection, the colours were as dark as blood and the shapes of the frozen stones were frightening and formless. The Anasazi Indians, the ones the Navajo call the 'Old People', had been here around the time the great cathedrals were being built in Europe, and they had left their marks on huge boulders by the side of the road. After the Anasazi Indians came the peoples from the north, among them the Navajo.

We drove up Highway 12 towards Window Rock.

'What', said Jack, 'is Window Rock?'

'It's the sort of headquarters of the Navajo,' said Suzan.

'You mean – like the Houses of Parliament?'

'Exactly.'

I was now in the passenger's seat deep in a book Suzan had bought on the way. It was called *Navajo – A Century of Progress*. It started with a letter from the chairman of the Navajo tribal council, a man called Raymond Nakai. The tone of his introduction and indeed of the binding and the typography of the book was that of the annual report of a large commercial company. Raymond, sounding a bit like John Major, ended his piece: 'There is much work yet to be done. The Navajo people will pause often during this centennial year to honour their heritage, but throughout all these events, we will be preparing to make this the start of a bold new era of progress, growth, self-sufficiency, industrial and economic development for our beloved country.' I wasn't sure whether he was talking about America or not.

But on the next page he moved in with a few sentences not usually found in the progress report issued by IBM or Metal Box.

> In the beginning (began Raymond), our Hataatli grandfathers tell us, there was darkness everywhere. And in

that underworld of darkness lived the insect people, at peace with one another.

But after a while, The People began to quarrel amongst themselves, and appealed to Tieholtsodi (Gatherer of Waters) to settle their differences. He decreed that they leave the land of darkness, and this the people did, through a small hole in the eastern sky.

This was more like it. Clearly, Raymond was just pretending to be an American. He was, deep down, a genuine Injun. The chairman's letter was obviously for the benefit of whoever was dishing out grants round here in north-east Arizona. When you got into the text, it was full of terrific stuff about the grasshopper people, and how the third world was coloured yellow, and Coyote had kidnapped Tieholtsodi's daughter.

As far as I could make out, the Navajo word for themselves – Dineh – meant the people. There was only one people, and that was them. I could identify with this. It is exactly how I feel. Or rather, how I *had* felt until I got off that plane. America, because of its startling capacity for change, is a country that encourages you to question your own identity. It was my 'little England' self that had been attracted to Nakai's book. The part of me that longed for the old ways. There was nothing new about it. Like those encyclopaedias I had read as a child in the 1950s, it preached the doctrine of limitless progress and, in one sense, its American-ness was not only skin deep, but as gloriously dated as that now dead decade. But there was despair here, too, and hopeless anger at the injustice of history.

What came off the pages of Nakai's report – in spite of the jaunty, anxious-to-please tone of most of it (one picture showed 'Ike' exchanging a joke with Dan Thornton, governor of Colorado, Ed Michim, governor of New Mexico, and a rather nervous-looking customer who turned out to be Sam Ahkeah, chairman of the Navajo tribal council) – was a story of cultural defeat, something an Englishman is only too well able to understand.

Towards the end of the book he told us how well the Navajo

47

were doing. How they were looking for oil, how they had got their own mounted police and chapter houses and community centres and roadside rest-stops and school bus shelters and offices of Navajo educational opportunity and the Navajo tourist museum. How there was a Visitor Centre now, and how General Dynamics and Fort Defiance kept The People busy. At the end of the book was a picture of four young Navajo in clean white shirts and respectable dresses holding school books labelled *Property of Window Rock School*. They looked happy, healthy and purposeful. But they looked like Americans, not Navajo. The Navajo story, as far as I could understand it, was a story of a people who only got the vote in 1924 (around the same time as English women – perhaps that was why Suzan identified with them so strongly) and had been forced into schools programmes, shot at by Colonel 'Kit' Carson, relocated, alcoholized and generally as much abused as all the other poor bastards thousands of miles over to the east, where now there is only corn and no buffalo. I sat up straight in the passenger's seat and folded my arms. 'Is now no buffalo,' I said in a sonorous voice. 'Is now no hunting for our people!' Suzan told me to shut up. Then she told Ned to put down his copy of the *Iliad* and take a look at the world around him. We were going to see the sacred place of the Navajo nation. I did not look to left or right as we drove, under a darkened sky, up the highway flanked by red earth towards a sign that said WINDOW ROCK. We passed a gas station that wasn't selling Navajo petrol, a hamburger stall that wasn't selling Navajo hamburgers, and a supermarket that looked like the kind of place you find out in Connemara on the west coast of Ireland – drab but well-stocked, a testament to a scattered community.

Everything in Window Rock is dull red. The earth around the buildings, the rocks, even the brick from which the buildings have been constructed, is a curious, unappetising shade of red that suggests the municipal. There was a Navajo youth centre and the Navajo Assembly Chamber, built like a hogan, the traditional Navajo dwelling, but they all reminded me of the low-rise, low-cost sheltered housing development you find somewhere off a road in the north of England.

There seemed, as far as I could tell, to be remarkably few Navajo about. Maybe they were all out organizing housing programmes or stacking the barrels of oil from the thousand wells on the reservation, or participating keenly in the harvest of some of the trees on the three-quarters of a million acres so vividly described by Raymond Nakai's book. Certainly the ones who were left behind seemed pretty depressed about it. There was a guy in a black stetson, a plaid shirt and jeans. He had the face of a warrior and the boots of a cowboy, but he didn't look as if the Navajo reservation or the United States of America were helping him into being in touch with either role. He was leaning up against a wall, staring at the street, a bleak expression on his face. Another guy in another stetson that looked as if it had been bought from the same store was standing on the highway holding up his thumb in a listless manner. An impromptu sign outside another of the red-brick buildings announced it was a Navajo youth centre. Youth centres, I thought to myself as I stood across the street staring at it, are for youths who have nothing to do.

There was a sign for a museum. I asked where it was but no one seemed to know. We walked up to the Navajo council chamber but there was no sign of the Navajo council. Maybe they were on holiday like everyone else. We drove back down the highway, and went into the Navajo tourist building where another man in a black stetson hat (maybe it belonged to the guy further down the street, and they took it in turns to wear it) told us the museum was back where we had come from.

In the museum there were more books. I bought two or three about the Navajo and a couple about the Hopi. There were a few glass cases, several black-and-white photographs and the odd display of pottery or arrows. On the wall there were pictures of Navajo in the past. One of them showed a group of Indians huddled together in cloaks. There was snow on the ground, and they looked listless and miserable. The caption said 'Bosque Redondo 1866'. There were pictures of hogans and a startling black-and-white image of Ganado Mucho (or Much

Cattle), who was the chief responsible for negotiating a successful peace with the whites. He had a fine, bronzed face, and in his left hand he carried a bow and arrow. About his shoulders was something that looked like a patterned carpet. On his head was what looked like a Confederate Army cap. He didn't look happy. When the Navajo were moved off their land to Bosque Redondo, their people started to suffer cold, hunger, disease and all of the things that killed off the American Indians just as effectively as General Custer did. What is extraordinary about their story is that they managed to talk their way back home. Not only that, they extorted a treaty from the US Government that is still the governing factor in their lives, a printed affirmation of their right to be in north-east Arizona. We know how far most such treaties were honoured.

Their real defeat was over the school question. It's a struggle recorded in Nakai's book, and it does not make pleasant reading. Children were torn from their parents and boarded out in a conscious attempt to make them Americans first and Indians second. And the Navajo, the most well-organized, flexible and – in the opinion of their Indian neighbours – ruthless peoples of the south west, were forced to trade their tradition of survival.

I got that ugly feeling again in Window Rock. Not the nausea I had on the *Back to the Future* ride, but a dull, hopeless, numb sense that all the beautiful places in America had been ruined.

'They screwed the Indians,' I said as we drove out of Window Rock.

'You mustn't call them Indians,' said Suzan. 'You have to say Native American these days!' I said I thought the term Native American was only another form of the brutal renaming and redefinition of territory that is still going on in the country. The Indian peoples of America owned the country long before Vespucci gave it its name. Why try and make them honorary citizens of a country they never wanted to belong to? All the council chambers and forests and oil wells and schools for the Navajo cannot bring back the time when they were Dineh, The People, and they went where they liked in their own place. Suzan said that that was more or less what she had meant by her last remark. She also asked me to please stop folding my arms and trying to look like Chief Running Cloud.

'Where's the hotel?' said Harry.

'It's in Chinle,' said Suzan. 'It's a Navajo hotel.'

'I thought,' said Ned, looking up from his copy of the *Iliad*, 'it was a Holiday Inn.'

'It's a Navajo Holiday Inn,' I said.

Which seemed to bring the conversation to a halt. As we drove through the bleak, arid outlands towards the Canyon de Chelly, over to our left you could see the edge of the painted desert, now dull and livid as more cloud piled up from the east. Thunder growled around behind us and, once, silent lightning as beautifully modelled as the veins of a leaf was printed on the bruised cloudscape.

Chinle is at the eastern end of the reservation, over towards the border with Colorado. It's laid out with a carelessness that seems natural to a country where there is so much space. One highway runs straight through it. We turned off by the signs to the canyon past a small parade of shops. About a mile down the road, flanked by excavators and spoil heaps of the red earth of Indian country, is the Holiday Inn.

I knew from the moment we turned into the parking lot that this was going to be unlike any other Holiday Inn I had ever visited. The small green board that said HOLIDAY INN in Holiday Inn handwriting didn't look quite real. It had the air of something being used on a Holiday Inn training course – a signpost from the 1950s that had done good work in its day, and had now been put out to grass. The low building that seemed to house the office and bar was built rather in the style of a Navajo council chamber, and when I pushed it open, I thought for a moment I had wandered into a gift shop. Hung from the ceiling were dolls, blankets and jewellery. Over the desk was a hand drawing of a Navajo in full dress, and next to it someone had printed the words:

Pow wow by the pool – 8.00 tonight

Behind the desk were two young Navajo women. I made the reservations and went out to the car.

'What are we doing here?' said Ned.

I found this question difficult to answer.

'There's a canyon here,' I said, 'like the Grand Canyon only smaller. And we're going to look at it. And there are Indians.'

Ned said he wished I would not talk to him as if he was eight years old.

'Where?' said Jack.

'Everywhere,' I said. 'Behind the bar, in the restaurant. Cleaning the rooms. Look. Over there. There's an Indian.'

A large Navajo woman was pushing a heavy truck of laundry across the courtyard.

'Right,' said Ned, 'we've seen her. Now can we go?'

I said we couldn't. We had booked into the Holiday Inn Chinle, and we were going to stay there. Ned said he didn't think he was.

'Don't then,' I said. 'Stay somewhere else. Stay in Tuba City or Moenkopi. Or Fort Defiance. I don't care.'

I lifted the bags out of the car and, slamming the door behind me, I stomped off towards the room. The room, like the Holiday Inn itself, was slightly sinister. There was a notice warning you to lock the doors and windows and to be careful of intruders. Although there was Holiday Inn soap and Holiday Inn shampoo and Holiday Inn furniture, Holiday Inn beds, they all looked somehow wrong, as if an alien civilization had tried to reconstruct such things from photographs or long-forgotten blueprints drawn up by the Holiday Inn management years ago. It was only when I went to the door that I saw the sign that read 'Administrated for Holiday Inns Ltd by Navajo Land Industries'. What was going on? Were the Navajo now Navajo plc like everything else in the world? And if they were, who ran Navajo plc? Was it simply a front organized for tribal clan structure? What had doing such un-Indian things as franchising an American hotel chain done to the family structure of The People? Were they all owned by the Japanese like everything else?

As I was asking myself these questions, Ned came in. He did not seem pleased to be here.

'I want,' he said suddenly, 'to go to Chicago.'

'Well you can't go to Chicago,' said Suzan, who, for some reason seemed to be equally out of temper, 'and that's that.'

'I want to go and see Lee,' said Ned.

And slamming the door behind him he went into the next room.

Ned is part of the Electronic Superhighway. He is well in with the Internet. He has something called a modem attached to his computer. The modem is attached to something called a bulletin board. On it he calls up other young people – some of whom, it appears, live in America. He had, without my being aware of it, made an arrangement to meet a young woman in Chicago at nine-thirty the following morning. I said that this was not really possible.

'Perhaps she has an imperfect knowledge of geography!' I said. 'Perhaps she just sits all day long glued to her computer waiting for people like Ned to get in touch!'

Ned asked me to explain this remark. I started to try.

'He's just being bloody awkward, that's what he is!' said Suzan.

Lee's father, a man called Nugent, had apparently had a long discussion with Ned and asked him over.

'He may be a pervert for all we know!' said Suzan. 'The whole family may be perverts! How can we send him halfway across America to a man called Nugent?'

'He can go to Nebraska and stay with someone called Hang Ching Chow as far as I am concerned,' I said. 'I don't care. I'm going to get a drink.'

Indian country was getting to me. I, too, slammed the door behind me as I clattered down the stairs and walked across to find Firewater Corner or whatever Navajo Land Industries had renamed the bar of the Holiday Inn at Chinle.

I couldn't see one anywhere. There were tables, set out with jugs of iced water and simple wooden chairs. There was a menu, advertising something called Navajo fried bread, which did not look promising, and over to the left was a buffet bar that for some reason reminded me of the buffet bar of the Havana Libra Hotel, Havana, Cuba.

I stayed in the Havana Libra Hotel some years ago, but I remember the buffet there as clearly as I recall the birth of my first child. I got to know it pretty well during the time I was there. It became part of my life. The first time I saw it, I was moderately excited by the sausage and the carrot salad, the aubergine dip and the beef stew and the coleslaw and the potatoes in oil and the mounds of sweet red pepper. The second time I saw it, I found it almost as attractive as the first time. But by the third or fourth time I looked at the same sausage, the same carrot salad, the same potatoes in oil and the same beef stew, the romance had gone out of them. By the second week, the buffet and I were in a state of smouldering tension. One of us, you felt, had to change or go. But the buffet did not change, and as there was very little else to eat in the Havana Libra Hotel, Havana, Cuba, I had nowhere to go. We went through a cold, loveless patch after that first week. I would go down, snatch a bit of sausage or hook out a few carrots as if I wanted to feel my pain. Some days I would ignore it completely. Sometimes I piled things furiously on to my plate whilst swearing at them under my breath. But in the end I could not escape it. I sat dutifully at the table and chewed my way through it hopelessly, furiously, as resigned as all the other poor bastards in the Havana Libra Hotel.

The buffet at the Holiday Inn Chinle had that air of quiet determination about it. I went over to the room clerk.

'I'd like a drink!' I said.

The room clerk handed me a menu. I could have diet cola or fresh fruit juice, water or iced tea or orange soda. I could not, however, see any sign of vodka, gin, sherry or –

No. At the bottom was something called O'Doul's lager.

'It'll be alcohol free,' said Suzan, a voice at my elbow. 'No alcohol is allowed on the Navajo reservation.'

I clutched at the handrail of the desk.

'None at all?' I said.

'None!' said a voice.

It was Jack, his eyes bright with amusement. Behind him came Harry. No sign of Ned.

'Is that right?' I said. 'Isn't that appalling?'

My voice was rising in pitch.

'They take their land, they force their children into schools, they don't even let the poor bastards have a drink!'

Suzan pointed out that it was the Navajo themselves who had banned alcohol. We were on Navajo territory, and the Navajo were telling us that while we were there we could not have so much as a shandy.

'I think that's disgusting,' I said. 'I think that's puritanical and narrow-minded and disgusting.'

I looked grimly round at the entrance hall.

'I mean if they don't want to drink, that's fine!' I went on. 'That's all very fine and dandy. If that's the way they want to lead their miserable lives, then OK. But I,' I was, I suddenly realized, prodding Suzan in the chest with my index finger, 'I would like a drink. Now.'

We went over to the tables and sat down.

'How far is the nearest off-licence?' I asked.

'About seventy-five miles,' said Jack.

There was a long pause.

'But you wouldn't be able to bring it on the reservation,' he went on. I said that was fine by me. They could stay there and watch the pow-wow by the pool. I would drive down to Highway 40 and buy a beer.

'Why don't you and Ned go to Chicago?' said Jack.

Harry looked worried about all of this. He doesn't like people arguing. When the waitress arrived I ordered something called a Navajo sandwich and a bottle of O'Doul's. On the label of the bottle, when it arrived, was a group of clean, well-dressed people enjoying bottles of O'Doul's. They were holding up O'Doul's. They were pouring it into glasses and mugs. Some of them were actually drinking it, others were in the grip of that delicious anticipatory glow. *Soon*, their faces said, *we will be getting the O'Doul's down us!* They looked as if they were trying to tempt people into a lot more than a glass of low-alcohol lager. A church perhaps, or some new country that needed well-dressed, polite, enthusiastic people who were prepared to work for nothing.

55

It tasted like fermented cardboard. I drank deeply.

From behind one of the houses around the hotel came the young woman I had seen earlier behind the desk. She was leading a group of children who were wearing a brave attempt at national costume. Some wore feathered headdresses, others the kind of blankets I had seen on pictures in the Navajo museum. Some were wearing jeans and T-shirts.

The young woman introduced herself as a party of plump Americans came in and occupied every other table in the place. 'Tonight,' she said, 'at our pool-side pow-wow, we will be doing some of the Navajo dances enjoyed by our people.' A middle-aged man in one of the regulation black stetsons walked onto the grass, sat down and began to bang a drum. An older man started to sing in a high, cracked voice. The children moved in a circle. They were severe as Irish step dancers, as their feet drove into the turf with the even force of hammer blows. One of the boys had his arms at full stretch. He shook to the music as if the wind was going through him.

'They're quite good!' said Harry.

'Not sure about the drummer,' said Jack.

'He's probably,' I said, 'been at the O'Doul's.'

There was a dance to celebrate a young girl getting married and a dance for rain, and there was a hunting dance. All these dances, as far as I could make out, were from other tribes. Quite a lot of them looked like the Navajo equivalent of headbanging. The coach party of American ladies beamed, as if the Navajo were a particularly promising bunch of lower infants.

Then there was a collection.

'Give them a lot,' said Harry, 'I feel sorry for them. Dancing for people like that.'

There was still no sign of Ned. The young woman asked if there were any questions. I asked if they knew any Navajo dances. The young woman smiled at me and said they couldn't possibly do them here. They only did them at night, she said.

One of the plump American ladies was busy setting up her own collection.

'Come on, give!' she said. 'Come on girls, let's have you!'

As the children started to dance again she waltzed out onto the lawn and seized one of the children by the hand. She did this with tremendous confidence. Were they, I wondered, a group of folk dance enthusiasts? The Indian child didn't seem to mind dancing with a middle-aged white woman.

More dollars piled up high on the plate. The young woman said that she and the rest of her party lived up behind the hill. She seemed to be trying to say they were attempting to keep Navajo traditions alive – but that it was an expensive business.

When the Navajo sandwich came, it turned out to be a hamburger. Outside it was something that tasted like sweet pitta bread. The plump ladies went over to the dancers. One lady put her arms around one of the children. Her friend took a picture of the two of them.

'Shall we take one of you?' said Jack. 'You could put your arm around the guy in the hat.'

I said I didn't want any photographs. I didn't understand any of this. I didn't know whether to be angry at the Indians or at the ladies in the coach party, at my family or at myself for coming all this way to gawp at something that I thought I had never hoped to understand. The old man was still sitting cross-legged on the ground, staring at it, as if it contained some extraordinary secret.

'That's enough Indians!' I said, as Ned came round the door of the restaurant. He seemed in conciliatory mood. Suzan, who was chewing her way through some Navajo fried bread, looked at me calmly.

'No, no,' she said. She wagged her finger at me, satirically. 'Tomorrow, the Hopi Indians! The Hopi! The Hopi!'

Ned joined us at the table. He seemed to be grinning at his mother. I didn't feel like grinning at anybody. I took a sip of O'Doul's and munched my Navajo sandwich. I was beginning to get some ideas of what the Hopi Indians might be like. None of these ideas suggested they might be worth the detour.

6

Even more reservations about even more Indians

In fact I was completely wrong.

The Hopi Indians turned out to be the most sensationally interesting bunch I have come across in the forty-six years I have spent on this planet.

Before heading out to see them, however, I set out to buy a black stetson. It was, I had decided, my only hope of blending in with the surroundings. In the courtyard of the Holiday Inn I had already seen four more men wearing them. And I had discovered, from one of them, that you could get them in a store on the road out of town. While I browsed through the hats (I take a size seven and three-quarters and Navajo heads seemed to stop in the low sixes) Ned bought a shirt and a pair of jeans. He had not, so far at any rate, mentioned Chicago. We went back into town, drove to the Visitor Centre at the edge of the Canyon de Chelly and asked to hire a guide to take us down into the canyon floor. I was given two or three forms to fill in, and told my guide would be waiting for me under a tree in the parking lot.

'How will I know who he is?'

'You'll know,' said the man behind the desk.

There was absolutely no doubt in my mind, when I caught sight of the plump, brown man sitting in the shade of a twisted tree, that this was an Indian guide. He was waiting in the way that suggests that no kind of time is necessarily more valuable than any other. His hands were folded on his knees and on his head was a black stetson.

'Hi!' he said, when I went up to him. 'My name's Clarence!'

I exchanged, in all, about a hundred and fifty words with Clarence. But, as they were spaced over a two-hour period, during which we walked down into the canyon that the Indians call

'Loose Sand Place', I feel he is probably my nearest thing to an acquaintance as far as the American Indians are concerned. But he was not a communicative man. He told me his grandfather had been on the forced march to Bosque Redondo. He also told me that the most important thing for a Navajo was which clan you belonged to. That was about all he told me. He didn't smile much either until, after a gruelling trip across the powdered sandy floor of the canyon, we made our way back to the cars, and he turned to me and said: 'Thirty dollars plus how much you enjoyed it.' I said I had enjoyed it fifteen dollars. He smiled then. Then we took the road south from Chinle, and then due west along Highway 264, through Keams Canyon. The Hopi live on a high, rocky plateau in the centre of the Navajo reservation. The climate is unfavourable – a few ragged attempts at cultivation, and soil strewn with off-white rock that looks about as conducive to agriculture as the surface of the moon, was all we saw. We drove down a steep road coming out of a ridge of cliffs that looked as if they had been carved out of dirty cement. Over to the south west we could see, in the distance, the painted desert, half aglow in the dim afternoon, and ahead of us a high arid place where the Hopi built their villages.

We were booked in at the Hopi Cultural Centre. The name had led me to expect an entrance hall like that of a provincial theatre in England, and that was almost what the place was like. But there was also the flavour of some other institution that at first I could not quite grasp. Was it an Old Folks' Home? A hospital? On the front desk was a cyclostyled sheet that read:

WELCOME TO SECOND MESA. THE CENTRE OF THE WORLD

There was no one behind the desk. I rang the bell. There was no response. Immediately to my left was a small plastic bookcase. Behind me was an army of wooden tables that looked as if they had been lifted from the Holiday Inn Chinle. For a wild moment I wondered whether the Hopi might possibly have caught up with the delights of gin and tonic or cool white Chardonnay. But there was no sign of a bar. There were a few other notices posted. One of them seemed to be saying that, from now on, no visitors would be allowed anywhere near something called the snake ceremony (I think it was a snake ceremony) at a place whose name suggested its inhabitants intended it to be unpronounceable as well as inaccessible. There was quite a lot of stuff, too, from a high-up in something called the Badger Clan – the general tone of which was that if you wanted to go and see the Hopi that was fine, but you had better remember to wipe your feet.

Perhaps this was a new approach to tourism, I thought.

DON'T BOTHER WITH HISTORIC BATH SPA.

DRIVE STRAIGHT PAST THE GREAT WALL OF CHINA.

And then something about the tone of the notices caught my attention. Chief whoever he was of the Badger Clan was making such a performance out of banning tourists from his ceremony because he felt bad about it. And it wasn't that 'This Hurts Me More Than It Hurts You' lie put out by schoolteachers as they offer people the cane. If you read the words carefully, you could see that he was genuinely distressed about giving whitey the thumbs-down. And not just that; although he was clearly some-one fairly high up in the food chain in Shungopovi or Moenkopi or Walpi or whatever his mesa was called, he wasn't issuing by-laws or edicts. There was a sense from the prose of a society that was more like a family than anything else. The Hopi didn't sound like Hopi plc or Hopi Ltd. I was listening to the authentic voice of an Indian tribe.

As I was thinking this, from around the corner came the fat-test woman I had ever seen. She was closely followed by a woman who was even fatter than she. Side by side or end to end, and it didn't really make much difference which way you mea-sured them, they measured at least eleven feet. They both seemed pretty cheerful about this.

'I wanted a room,' I said.

The fattest of the two said:

'You're English. I love the Beatles.'

It was nice to meet someone who had heard of the Beatles, even if I had to travel over 5,000 miles to do so. Whenever I men-tion the Beatles to my children (who were marching into the Hopi Cultural Centre behind their mother) they look at me with studied sympathy.

'I also like the Beatles!' I said.

I felt I was back in 1968, hitch-hiking around Europe with only a guitar and the chords to *Norwegian Wood* between me and loneliness and starvation.

'One room!' she said.

Suzan had come in and was standing a little way away from us, listening to this conversation.

'If you think we'll all fit into one room … ' I said.

The fat woman looked at us. We must have seemed pretty insubstantial to her.

'You'll easily fit!' she said. 'I'll give you a roll-away.'

Suzan stepped forward.

'We want to look at a Hopi village,' she said, 'and we were wondering which ones we were allowed to go into.'

The two women looked at each other. The thinner of the two said:

'You can go to First Mesa. At eleven in the morning. Someone will take you round.'

'We're interested', said Suzan, slightly shyly, 'in Kachinas.'

The woman's eyes clouded over slightly.

'Yes,' she said. 'Yes.'

Then –

'You may buy things there!' she said.

I thought her manner had changed slightly.

'Kachina dolls,' said Suzan to me, 'they make dolls.'

'Fine,' I said.

I had bought two books – one called *Pages from Hopi History* by one Harry C. James, the other *The Book of the Hopi* by Frank Waters. On my way out to the car to get the luggage I took a look around the centre. Everywhere were crudely duplicated notices like the one I had seen by the desk. On one of the doors was a notice fixed there by something called the Hopi Tribal Council. While Suzan and the others went into something at the back called the Badger Craft Shop, I tried to find out a little more about the tribe I was visiting. I started with Harry C. James.

One thing was clear. They were not good Americans. I liked

them for that. They were suspicious of all Americans – even the liberal ones. Even, as far as I could make out, people like Harry C. James, who devoted his life to getting down with the Coyote Clan and boning up on Chief Tewaaquaptewa, were of far less interest to them than their own culture and history.

The Hopi Tribal Council had been formed in 1936 after a series of meetings between people like James and the Hopi, who had talked for days about the question of whether they should have such a thing. They had clearly not got as far as running up an architect-designed building to house the thing. In fact, at one point, James showed slight traces of peevishness when discussing it. 'Even now,' he remarked, 'in 1974, it is only functioning about as well as can be expected.' Clearly the tatty bits of paper glued to doors, stained with badly duplicated ink, were a sign of strength, not of weakness. These guys did not give a stuff for Jeffersonian democracy. With them it was straight to the clan father to find out what Coyote did to the parrot god after the thunder god slew the wolves with the thunderbolt.

The really mind-boggling thing about the Hopi (the thing that drew the unwelcome attention of the hippy communities in the late 1960s) is that they have not been divorced from that most sacred and important item on the agenda of the American Indians – residence in the place which their history makes sacred. The Hopi Cultural Centre might be as artificial as a can of O'Doul's lager, but unlike its counterpart over on the Navajo reservation, it did not express, could not express, the real aspirations of the people that it was supposed to represent. These mesas, or villages, as I read in James's book, were continuously inhabited, clan-based settlements that reach back hundreds of years to when the first settlers reached these high plateaux.

Except – when did they get here? Had they come with the Navajo? Or before? They seemed to share the same taste in motel decor, but apart from that, how did they get along with the people over at the Canyon de Chelly?

A large saloon car was pulling up outside. Two very fat policemen got out. On the side of the car I managed to read the words HOPI TRIBAL POLICE in gold letters.

'This,' said a voice at my elbow, 'is weird.'

It was Ned. He seemed to have forgotten all about Chicago. He was wearing a sombrero that he had bought at Universal Studios. Somewhere along the way he had bought a bootlace tie to go with the shirt he had acquired in Chinle. All he needed, I thought to myself, was a pair of leather boots and he would be indistinguishable from the local cowboys. Except, of course, there was still something ineradicably European about him. And it wasn't just his glasses. His pale face looked puzzled.

'The distinguishing feature of the Hopi,' said Jack in a low voice as we headed for the room, 'seems to be that they are fat.'

This was certainly true of the ones in the Hopi Cultural Centre. I had never seen so many fat people in my life. The receptionist was fat. The chambermaids were fat. The waiters and waitresses were fat. The guests were fat. The two policemen, who were now sitting drinking enormous Diet Cokes at one of the tables, were fatter than any of them.

'They are,' said Suzan, 'they are *huge*!'

'You should blend in well with them then!' said Ned to Harry. Jack laughed coarsely. Harry hit him. We went to our room and watched a chat show in which relatives confronted family members who had tried to kill them. It was presented by a small blonde woman, whose appetite for human misery seemed inexhaustible.

'Dinner!' said Ned eventually, as he staggered out of the room holding his head. 'There's fuck all else to do in this place!'

I went into dinner, clutching *Book of the Hopi*, by Frank Waters.

All around the room very fat people were drinking very large colas and iced tea out of gigantic paper cups. Two very, very fat waitresses were serving them. As I read on through Frank Waters' book, I could not connect what I was reading with what I was seeing.

'They have Hopi fried bread here!' said Harry. 'I expect it's just like Navajo fried bread.'

I didn't answer. I was reading. The Hopi cosmology has the edge on the Old Testament. For a start they don't have one world but four. And the Hopi, who like everyone else are the heroes of their own theology, travel through them not – as in Hesiod's 'Theogeny' or the Bible's 'Exodus' – getting worse but, rather cheeringly, getting better. Their worlds are stacked on top of each other like apartments in a building, and the Hopi start at the bottom with a group called the Ant People. They work their way up to our world (the present one) and then, after crossing some stepping stones across the ocean, fetch up in America. There is a flood, a rather unpleasant character called Spider Woman, and then there are the Hopi's travels inside America. Hopi myth describes them in an amazingly detailed way, travelling south, north, west and east in the shape of the swastika, following the line of the Rockies north and swinging back down into California, moving into South America and back up north in order to fulfil a divinely ordered sequence of migrations. What is weird about it is that they seem to have left traces of their passage in all the places referred to in their stories, from Winslow, Arizona to Yucatán, Mexico. It seems most likely that they are a people as old as the Aztecs or the Maya.

'Two Diet Cokes, an iced tea, an orange soda and a regular Coke!' said the almost spherical Hopi waiter as he arrived at our table.

I looked at him. He was wearing a loose-fitting blue boiler suit that looked as if it had been given to him by Texaco. It was hard to believe that he was probably a distant relative of Atahualpa and all those other guys who rolled over for Cortez 300-odd years ago. I ordered a Hopi stew.

'Is that book interesting?' said Harry.

'It is,' I said.

I didn't look up until the stew arrived. It was brought by a different, but equally fat, member of the staff.

'Tell me,' Suzan asked him, 'I saw something called the Badger Art Gallery. What time does it open?'

The man didn't appear to know.

'He probably isn't a member of the Badger Clan,' I said, when he had gone. The stew was small, gritty bits of lamb in a kind of barley broth. It tasted quite pleasant. They were all looking blankly at me.

'The Badger Clan,' I said in the knowledgeable tones of one who has only recently acquired a fact, 'is one of the four most important Hopi clans. A number of clans, led by the Bear Clan, were involved in the wanderings through South America, but on their way back one of their children fell sick, and Honani the badger cured her. So from then on they were known as the Badger Clan.'

Jack, who had his teeth stuck into the Hopi hamburger, looked at me doubtfully.

'Are you feeling OK?' he said.

'The Badger Clan,' I went on, 'settled in Mexico, then at the Canyon de Chelly, which, as I am sure you are aware, is known by the Indians as Loose Sand Place, and then –'

'They formed a small, string orchestra!' said Ned.

He had chosen the Hopi stew. He did not seem particularly thrilled with it.

'It's fantastic,' I went on, waving the book at them. 'This guy found an old man at the Badger Clan called John Lansa who took him to a place in the Mesa Verde where he *predicted* they'd see some drawings told of in the Hopi myths, hundreds of years ago! Proving their myths aren't just stories! They're actual descriptions of real migrations made thousands of years ago!'

I could see I was losing my audience. They didn't care about the Hopi, I said. They had no poetry in their souls. They were not interested in the words of Male Followed By Butterfly Maiden or White Cloud Above Horizon or, for that matter, what Mrs Besse Sakmosi or Chasing One Another On Green Field had to say.

'We're tired,' said Suzan, 'that's all.'

'Anyway,' said Jack, 'I don't think there are any of those Indians left here.' He pointed to an enormous man in glasses devouring his evening meal.

'He's more Just Devoured A Whopper-Burger, or Grease Running Down Chin From Too Many French Fries.'

I folded the book and placed it, face down, on the table. Maybe one of the Hopi would spot I was reading it and engage me in conversation. As I chewed on the lamb I looked round the dining room. Most of the people there were distinctly Hopi in appearance. The Hopi features are quite unlike the Navajo, who they call Tavasu – or He Who Pounds Your Head. When not inflated to sixteen stone they do have an Aztec elegance. And something else, too. A woman opposite me, who looked as if she was visiting from the city, glanced about her sharply. She had a slightly furtive expression that I associate with a certain kind of intelligence.

'They're inscrutable,' I said, 'that's what they are.'

Their food was certainly inscrutable. It did not give much away in the flavour line. I tried to tell myself, as I crunched through my blue corn chips, that they were not simply food. They were of ritual significance. In the olden days, when a child was born its corn-mother, an ear of wheat, was placed next to it, where it was kept for twenty days. Corn is sacred to the Hopi who, unlike the Navajo, are farmers, peaceful people.

It didn't make the corn chips taste any better.

I abandoned the Hopi stew. After a coffee, the five of us went through to the Badger Art Gallery. It was a small room at the back of the hotel where Kachina dolls were arranged, like toy soldiers on glass shelves. Kachinas are spirits who run between this world and the world of the gods, and from time to time leap like Superman into north-east Arizona to give the Hopi a hand. Most of the time the Kachinas zoom around on top of the San Francisco mountain near Flagstaff. The Kachina dolls are not, themselves, Kachinas, and have no ritual significance. They are used simply to educate Hopi children in the ways of their religion.

I didn't really like the art gallery. It was difficult to connect it with what I had been reading. Waters's book was printed in 1974; maybe since he finished it the 'friendlies' of the Hopi, those who favour contact with the white man and who, unsurprisingly, have ended up running the tribal council, had won. Maybe, like the Navajo, their culture had lost the battle with rapacious, xenophobic whites. When we trudged back to the room to lie, as we had lain so often before on this trip, in three beds in a long line, I felt depressed.

'Tomorrow,' said Suzan, 'you'll see the real thing. We'll go to

First Mesa. And you'll see the Hopi. For real.'

I switched on the television. I did not answer.

'It'll be amazing,' said Suzan, 'I promise.'

7

Walpi

Walpi, on First Mesa, is high on a rock at the eastern end of Hopi territory. It is close to Keams Canyon, where the Hopi's Indian agents were based, and where in the late nineteenth century the obligatory school was founded. Walpi is where the Navajo Tiponis – their sacred objects – were kept after the Navajo retreat from Bosque Redondo, and although it is not the oldest continuously inhabited settlement in the United States (Oraibi nearby has that distinction), people have been living there at least since the middle ages. For those who live in Walpi, at the western end of the Mesa – a place you can only visit escorted by a guide – there is no electricity and no running water.

They don't need electricity or running water. They were asked if they wanted it and they said no. They have Masaow, the creator of all things, and they have the Kachinas, and they have feather bunches – *pahos* or prayer bundles – which they use to pray to their gods.

Next morning we went back along the road and took the steep way up the hillside. There were eight or nine other cars parked in the town square. We waited for our tour guide in a large empty room. On the walls were posters telling us that we were at risk from the Hanta virus, and that we should be careful not to get too friendly with the local rats. There was another poster that was about the dangers of alcohol, and another, a black-and-white picture of a young girl alone on a bed, that hinted that somebody thought that the Hopi might be given to child abuse.

Suzan found a yellowed news clipping that gave an account of a recent law suit. Apparently the Hopi were suing the Navajo over a land claim. I didn't quite see how this squared with the Hopi ideal of being at one with all peoples across the face of the

68

earth, and listening to the spirit of their creator Taiowa, who had allowed his spirit to come out through the soft spot on the top of the head (kopavi). Why couldn't they just cast a spell on the bastards, as in the old days?

Then, from a room at the back, came a severe-looking woman in glasses. She looked, I thought, a bit like a provincial schoolteacher. She sat at a table and started to fill in what looked like an official form.

'Hi!' I said.

She nodded. She didn't smile.

'What time does the tour start?'

'Half an hour.'

She still didn't smile. Two or three more people came into the room. Outside, on the step, was an old Hopi woman. She was sitting in the pale sunlight, and stretched out at her feet was a dirty newspaper on which were two Kachina dolls. I suddenly remembered that it was Suzan's birthday.

I am not in the habit of forgetting her birthday. I have only done it once. She was very good about it. She didn't grab a piece of lead piping and club me over the head and shoulders – however, there were times in the week or so that followed when I wished she had. I would have welcomed a good kicking, or indeed anything that smacked at some level of communication. But, on this trip, places and people were moving so fast past me that I had simply forgotten that today was July 27th.

I went out to the Hopi woman and asked her about the dolls. She picked up one. It was about six to eight inches high. It had a shaggy head, two vestigial arms, and on the trunk was a kind of green wash on which was painted a vivid fork of lightning. It recalled, in the immediate spirit of naive art, the flash we had seen on the road out of Window Rock.

'Twenty-five dollar,' she said. 'My son did it.'

I bought it. The Hopi woman wrapped it in newspaper. And then I went back in and gave it to Suzan.

'Happy birthday!' I said.

'Thanks!' she said. I grinned encouragingly at the woman behind the table.

'It's my wife's birthday!' I said.

I thought this might give some anthropological significance to the rather grubby transaction that had just gone on outside the town hall.

'Cute!' said the woman, in a voice that suggested it was anything but.

Outside was a large notice that told us that we were not welcome beyond it unless accompanied by a Hopi guide. At eleven o'clock, the Hopi woman behind the table got up without looking at any of us, and walked out into the square. While we had been inside the hall a few other tourists had arrived. A large Ford was bouncing up the road, driven by a smart-looking woman in a headscarf. I watched the woman from the town hall. When she got to the middle of the square, she stopped, turned and said in a listless voice –

'You may now follow me to visit the old village of Walpi, on First Mesa. You may not take photographs, but if you wish you may buy pottery or craft.'

There were now about ten people in the group. We followed the woman along a narrow track that followed the crest of the ridge on which Walpi is built. On either side of us white rock fell away sharply. On the right we were looking across at the seemingly endless plains – the huge expanse of arid earth and treeless stone. This, I thought to myself, is the only reason the Hopi are still here. Their land isn't worth enough to the white man. Immediately below us, about 200 yards down the cliff, we could see rotting piles of vegetables, a stew of bottles on dirty newspapers, and some crazily-dismembered chairs.

'Hopi refuse disposal!' said Jack.

I was trying to get close to the woman to let her know that I wasn't your ordinary tourist. In fact last night in bed I had become something of a world-class expert on the Hopi. Until three in the morning I had read the *Story of a Hopi*, *Tales of a Hopi*, *Book of the Hopi*, *Hopi Cultural Myths*, *Hopi Life*, and *The Hopi Snake Dance Ritual* by Dr Sheila Galagher of the University of Northern Arizona, the *Ways of the Hopi*, *Travels among the Hopi*, *Some Stories of the Hopi* and at least two or three other short pamphlets. I fell in step with her as we made our way out to the eastern tip of the mesa. What was the best way, I wondered, to break the ice?

'During Wuwuchim, the ... er ... first great winter festival which begins the ceremonial year with the ... er ... the celebration of the three phases of creation, I imagine you are all pretty excited!'

The woman looked at the ground as she walked. Over by one of the low stone houses, a bit like sheep pens, we passed a tiny, ragged boy sitting in the dirt. He was playing a Gameboy. I simply couldn't think how to get her going.

'The great Kiva, the twelfth-century monument found at Aztec, New Mexico, is very like your Kivas here on Walpi, isn't it?'

We were getting closer and closer to the heart of the old village. I was going to have to move fast. Finally, as we came out into the square at the far end of the ridge, I made my move.

'Kachinas,' I said, 'are kind of spirits, aren't they?'

She looked at me pityingly. It was as if I had just told her I believed in Father Christmas.

'Yes,' she said.

And then she added: 'You may also buy Kachina dolls from the houses here.'

It takes rather longer than two to three hours to clue yourself into the ritual life of an Indian tribe. Even Kevin Costner presumably did not offer a prayer mat and ritual slab of tobacco twenty minutes after making the acquaintance of a new lot of Native Americans. It takes years. You have to do the groundwork. You can't do it on half a Viking paperback.

The woman showed us the Kiva – the prayer house – in the plaza that stretches out at the eastern end of the village. In keeping with their story of how the world was made, the Hopi set great store by climbing out of their churches by a ladder through a hole in the roof that mimics their ascent to the better world above. The idea that you can make a story true by re-enacting it ought not to be a difficult one for someone raised in the Christian tradition to absorb. But the Kiva is on the lively side

71

for a sacred building. It isn't just wafers and a few measly rations of communion wine. Quite a lot of pipe smoking goes on down there. There is even a rather thrilling-sounding whipping ceremony, although, as far as I could make out from Oswald Whitebear Fredericks, they haven't really been into S & M since about 1934.

'This,' said the woman, 'is a kiva – which is a place where religious ceremonies are held.' That was it. Not a word about what really went on. Not a word about them taking off all of their clothes and drenching each other in water. Not a word about the fact that, during the mystery plays that are still performed by the villagers, excited youths jump down into the kiva through the roof with lighted torches and scare the shit out of everyone down there. Not a word about the antics of the Two-horn Clan or the mimic ritual sacrifice that echoes a real sacrifice which must have been carried out not so very long ago. I thought my own performance, when taking a group of American ladies to visit Stratford-upon-Avon in the summer of 1968 was rather better. As a tour guide, our lady was about as exciting as a meal at the Hopi Cultural Centre. I thought of tempting her out with a few aperçus about the significance of the Coyote Clan and the history of old Oraibi, but before I could do so, she was hoofing it off back to the Walpi town hall at a fair lick. She just couldn't wait to get back among those Hanta virus posters, drafting out a few more tough memos for the Hopi tribal council about how to keep white boys in their place.

As we moved away from the square I saw, on a rough pile of stones a few yards away from the kiva, a packet of grubby feathers and a few scraps of thick, coarse grass. It was tied with string and was hidden behind a heavy stone. I didn't like to touch it. There was something sad about it – a small effort at control over the harsh plain that stretched below and all around us. There was something angry and hopeless, too, like a child writing I HATE MY DADDY on the wall of his bedroom, or kicking the leg of a chair because it fell against him and hurt his leg. There was also – and this I couldn't quite explain – something furtive and shameful about it. Why do prayers have to be secret? And then I thought – *the shame comes from me, the white man.*

The Hopi, like the Aztecs, have a myth of a lost white brother whom they call their pahana. When the first Spaniard arrived, in 1540, the Hopi went down to meet him, but, unlike Atahualpa the Inca, they knew that Pedro (for such was the Spaniard's name) was not he. The Bear Clan leader extended his hand palm up to the man; if he slapped his palm down on it in a gesture of friendship (presumably shouting the Hopi equivalent of 'Gimme five bro' as he did so) they knew he was their long-lost white brother. As it was, Pedro had assumed the native was after money and all of his men had dropped something into the Hopi's open palm. From this moment, Hopi stories tell us, they knew the Spaniards were a dodgy lot. They turned and went back to their village. If they had had any idea that the Spaniards were going to spend the next hundred years doing things like dowsing the Incas in burning turpentine, they might have been rather less restrained in their disapproval. As we all stood in the main square of the village, I thought about how I, too, was a long way away from being anyone's lost white brother. I thought about how stupid and vulgar and simplistic the Christian religion can be. How can one possibly have faith in something that takes no account of what is at the heart of the Hopi, and indeed of all Indian religious myths, the relationship with the immediate environment in which one finds oneself? It is this divorce from the natural world that justifies the Christian's cruelty in so many respects – to its animals, its seeds, plants and forests. I thought about my father, whose own father was vicar of a church in Wales, and wondered what comforted him as he lay dying on his hospital bed in north London. Was it the thought of eternal life and being with Jesus? I don't think so. I think it was more likely to be the sight of a tree slowly coming into leaf on a bleak lawn on the other side of his hospital window.

The woman walked about ten or fifteen yards ahead of us as we went back through the village. A little girl leant out of a door offering us a Kachina doll. Suzan looked at it, smiled, thanked the girl, handed it back and passed on. Then we filtered into a darkened room in which a plump, grinning young man of about twenty was setting out five or six beautifully worked wooden Kachina dolls on a table covered with a thick plastic cloth. They were each made from a single piece of cottonwood. They had the look of warriors or earth mothers, something far more primitive and alien than the stuff we had seen in the shop at the Hopi Cultural Centre.

The young man said 'Welcome!'

It was a simple, peasant interior of the kind you might see in Greece or parts of southern Spain. But beyond him I could see a tape deck, and fixed to a notice board behind his head were postcards that seemed to come from all over the world. Also, to his right, was a telephone. We were obviously back in new Walpi.

'We Hopis believe that we live at the centre of the world and are in harmony with it. This is why you have come to see us and why we do not leave here!'

I goggled at him. Since coming to America I had not met anyone who talked quite like this. If I have made him sound a little like a hippy vicar it is only because I have not been able to remember his words very precisely. What was obvious, though, was that he was translating some very complicated and deeply felt philosophical ideas about the world that were closer to mediaeval mysticism than the easy platitudes you find at the showbiz end of Western religion.

'All men are our brothers,' he said, 'and we wish them peace and happiness, and also to the earth, the sun and the stars – also our brothers.'

Again, this is not an exact transcription of what he said. Looking at it on the page it may look like an excerpt from a warm-up act at Las Vegas. Perhaps this is only because the young man was obviously somebody who had spent a lot of his time trying to get his culture into a form where it could be easily assimilated by the average American tourist. It certainly did not square with what I had been getting from Oscar Oswald Whitebear Fredericks or Ralph Selaner (Place In Flowers Where Pollen Rests) or the late Otto Pentiwa (Painting Many Kachina Masks).

'This', he said, holding up a beautifully-carved wooden figure that looked a little like a Japanese Samurai warrior, 'is made by my uncle, whose work has been exhibited with great success in New York. It is a picture of the corn-goddess who is the bringer of fruit and food to the Hopi.' He grinned round at us in a friendly fashion. It was difficult not to like him. But it was very, very difficult to relate what he said or the way in which he said it to the bare plateau or the ancient huddled stone houses and the village a few yards down to our east. Perhaps he had been flown in from the Hopi Cultural Centre.

'I have my friends,' he said (He Whose Uncle Has Been Exhibited With Great Success In New York), 'all over the world. They ring me, and I talk to them in the middle of the night. We talk because when they have been with us they want to know how to live. We, the Hopi, teach that those who are at peace in their hearts are in the great shelter of life and, you see, from humble people, from little nations, there is much to learn. You can read this in the earth itself. Plant forms from previous worlds are beginning to spring up as seeds. The same kind of seeds are being planted in the sky as stars. And seeds are planted in our hearts. Don't you think?'

'Right,' said Suzan, in a low, serious voice.

She was picking up one of the Kachina dolls. The man at the other end of the line, his arms folded, glanced quickly towards it. Then he composed his face, to show that he too knew how to be serious before discussing something as vulgar as money. My wife has extremely good taste. Before the man over to my left unclasped his arms, I said swiftly –

'How much?'

'Seventy dollars!' said He Whose Uncle Has Been Exhibited With Great Success In New York.

'Very reasonable!' I said.

And before the man could protest at this violation of the sacred relationship between the inhabitants of First Mesa and the dedicated tourists who beat a path up their remote cliff face and fork out hundred-dollar bills, He Whose Uncle Has Been Exhibited With Great Success In New York had done the deal. He probably, I thought, had a machine for franking your Access card somewhere under the table.

It's a weird figure. Although it carries sheaves of corn on either side, it has a strangely military aspect. The pale wood is very finely carved and beautifully finished. It's standing on my desk now. Somewhere in one of the drawers of the desk is a visiting card on which is the telephone number of the young man whose uncle made it. His uncle, of course, isn't what we would call an uncle. The Hopi are matrilineal. He would simply be an older man who had taken an interest in someone who seemed as interested as he in the old ways and the old religion. There are days when I think I am going to pick it up, dial a long number and find myself talking to First Mesa, a village whose people and culture are as old as the Incas. But every time I reach for the phone, I think of the money. I wonder what I'm going to say to the guy, and I wonder whether anything will ever make a bridge between the white men and those strange, quietly-spoken people who live high up on a lonely plateau, miles away from anywhere, in what they call the centre of the world.

8

Place of many people with video cameras

The last stop north-east as you leave the Navajo reservation and head towards the Grand Canyon (a tourist resource which the US government has not yet thought fit to give back to Navajo plc) is the Cameron Trading Post. In spite of the pleasant walled garden at the rear, it still has the feeling of something designed by someone who thinks this is how Indians ought to live. Even if he was an Indian. It's made of the same red brick as the Navajo Assembly Rooms at Window Rock, and although there are fig trees and a lattice of vines across the place, it has a sterile, dead atmosphere. In the lobby are mass-produced Kachina dolls which the enterprising Navajo manufacture for the tourists. For the Hopi it must be a bit like a Catholic priest walking into a religious relic store called 'Rosenbaum and Finkelkraut – We Sell Crucifixes'.

Ned, Jack and Harry were eager to leave the reservation.

'I feel sorry for all of them,' Harry said, 'the Navajo and the Hopi. And I want to see the Grand Canyon.'

He pulled his baseball cap down over his eyes.

'But I don't want to fall into it.'

'You won't,' I said, 'they have rails round it.'

We were sitting in our room looking out at the straight road that runs up through the Cameron Trading Post from Monument Valley. There was a shabby, iron bridge over the Colorado river – the water of which seemed to be dark green. From time to time a car thudded past on the lonely road. Beyond, the Painted Desert glowed quietly in the evening light.

'Just think,' said Harry, 'this time tomorrow we'll be back on American territory.'

Leaving the Navajo reservation is a bit like checking out of

East Berlin back in the early 1980s. The road surface improves. The vegetation acquires a prosperous bourgeois air. People in the car become noticeably less serious.

As we drove up towards the eastern end of the southern rim of the Grand Canyon, there was also quite a bit of excitement. Several people at Gavin Simpson's pool-side brunch had told me what I might expect to feel when I first saw the Grand Canyon. They were men and women who were paid something in excess of $100,000 a throw for knowing what people might be expected to feel, and there were moments, as they described the emotions I was about to undergo, when I felt determined not to experience any of them.

'It is *awesome*,' a man called (I think) Lolla had said. 'It does things to your mind!' said a girl called (I think) Roger. But it was Gavin Simpson, as usual, who put his finger on it. He is not paid $300,000 a picture for nothing.

'Nigel,' he had said, putting a strong hand on my shoulder, as I tried hard to prepare my small, grovelling English soul for the experience, 'it is *big*!'

Even Gavin Simpson, however, had not prepared me for what I saw, quite by accident, as we drove up towards the southern rim. I had been primed by people other than Simpson and his merry men. At a small wooden hut a woman in a Canadian Mountie's hat, as seen in the Yogi Bear cartoons, had offered us a three-day pass. On the main road up we had seen cars coming from the other direction, driving slowly, their passengers craning their necks behind them as if they were being followed by an unfriendly prehistoric animal of some size.

But my first sight of the canyon came on me, unexpectedly, as we turned a corner of the steep road. Over to my right, a long, long way away, I caught sight of the beginnings of a deep gash in the earth's surface. I couldn't understand how far away it was. It was obviously the far side of the canyon, but there was something not right about the ground between me and what must be the edge closest to me. All I had a chance to see, at first, was an intricately-worked section of cliff face which, because it was cast in earth as red and alive as cooked clay, caught the morning sun and gave it back to me in more shades between pink and crimson than I knew existed. But I also had the chance to realize that if, *if* – (and now we were swinging away south, away from the edge) – *if* what my eye told me about the distance between us and the northern rim was in any way correct, then, once again, Gavin Simpson had gone straight to the heart of a great experience. This thing was … well … big. Quite amazingly, colossally, stupendously, astonishingly, surprisingly … BIG.

And no sooner had I got to the realization that what the Grand Canyon was not was a super-large hole in the ground, we had swung back north again and I was looking at more and more and more frozen waterfalls of red rock. But the word 'red' does not begin to describe the thousands of shades between brown and magenta that tumble thousands of feet down from the Arizona hills to the Canyon's depths where, miles in the distance, the Colorado river twists in mean subjection to the heights it must have helped to carve out of the ancient rock. And then we had swung away from the road yet again and lost sight of the thing, but just as we were gaining speed and thinking, yes, we have shaken it off, it had thrown itself round like a dragon's tail, and it lay once more in our path. Now, however, it was a monster unmasked, Tyrannosaurus Rex letting rip a thousand-fanged smile for the tourists' cameras. And, at the next bend, it let us see what it had, smack in the face. A crude, Brobdingnagian strip-tease gave us an eyeful of ochre, a socking great major chord of stone and sun, as if Helios himself had been buried, long ago, in this very place, and had only just at that moment made it to the surface for our benefit.

Jack was making a gurgling noise in the back. Ned stiffened in his seat and allowed his copy of William Empson's *Seven Types of Ambiguity* to fall, unheeded, to the floor.

'Camera!' he croaked, in a low voice. 'Camera!'

Next to me, Suzan looked for, and failed to find, the right word to describe what we had just seen. Harry looked more than usually wide-eyed.

'How close do we go to it?' he said, in a carefully controlled voice.

The road took another turn, and suddenly the Grand Canyon was no longer the Grand Canyon, but a tourist attraction. Ahead was the car park, a restaurant, an observation tower, a brace of coin-operated telescopes and, by a railing at the Canyon's edge, a small Japanese man who had been video-recorded by a group of three other Japanese men.

We got out of the car, went to the rail and looked at the Canyon.

It had not got any smaller. But there were a lot of things designed to help you try and come to terms with it. There was a noticeboard that told you how it had all got there. It mentioned volcanic eruptions and glacial development and the Jurassic (or was it the Mesozoic) era. It told you how many miles it was wide, and how many miles deep, and how it was bigger than any other silicated alluvial fault known to man. There were contour maps and elevations and, near them, interesting facts about how the local Indians had helped the first Spaniards to come across it as they passed this way heading south, looking for gold.

But none of the explanations explained it. The Grand Canyon defies explanation. It combines intricacy and grandeur so cleverly, and is so uncompromised by its own scale, that it is almost impossible to believe that the thing isn't as deliberately calculated an artefact as the Pyramids or the Eiffel Tower.

That illusion was heightened, for me, by the fact that, as we drove along the southern rim to Grand Canyon village, every observation point was swarming with French, Italian, Chinese, Japanese, English, Spanish and every other kind of tourist, all of them clicking cameras and posing by the rail with their children, as if they had personally captured and killed this prime geological specimen.

I wanted to walk down into it.

'I think,' Suzan said slowly, 'it is rather larger than you think.'

I said I would walk a small distance down it and then come back. At an observation point just before Grand Canyon village – a collection of hotels, car parks, coaches and restaurants at about the centre of the southern rim – I found a path which went steeply down into the Canyon. There was a line of donkeys jostling up towards us. A sign told anyone interested that if they wanted to hike down to the river, they would need about a gallon of water if they weren't going to die of dehydration. A plump lady sweated up towards me along the stony path. She was carrying an empty bottle of Evian water.

'Don't do it,' she said, 'it wasn't worth it.'

I went down the track past the donkeys. Behind me I heard Suzan say to Ned:

'He's going down into the Canyon!'

There was a lot of muttering from the rest of the family. Another middle-aged lady forced her way up the path from the Canyon.

'He's going down!' Jack called to Ned. 'He's off!'

'You can't trust him!' Suzan was shouting. 'I *knew* he'd do this!'

Anyone would have thought I was proposing to paraglide off the edge. I went on down the track. It curved back into the cliff face. The drop to my immediate right went thousands of feet sheer down to the valley floor. I stopped and looked across to the river. I looked up at the Canyon's rim and saw my wife and three sons leaning down towards me anxiously.

People huddle together in families, I thought to myself as I looked at the acres of bleached stone below me, precisely because the earth is as inhospitable as this. If the kingdom is, as Augustine said, a piece of highway robbery, then the family is the primal, criminal cell. Societies who don't have a well-ordered incest taboo perish. And travel is, in a sense, a ritual assertion of that taboo, an attempt to proceed from the known to the unknown. But I, unlike the proper traveller, was journeying with both wife and children, unable to survive easily for long without the comforting stench of immediate relations.

I stood, looking back up at them. If anyone, I reflected, was giving off a comforting stench, it was me. The sweat was leaking down under my glasses and over the reddened bulbous end of my nose. Sweat was growing from under my hairline across my

81

forehead. Sweat was moving on from armpit to thigh, from shoulder blade to buttocks. I wondered how I looked to them. I recalled my own father. He seemed to change style and shape with every mood. Sometimes he was a stern, Victorian cut-out, sitting by the fire in our suburban house, a French paperback novel in his hand; and sometimes a small, twinkling gnome cracking jokes and smiling smiles. And then he was stretched out on a hospital bed, his mouth horribly ajar, his tiny shrunken cheeks pale as the rocks around me. A father's moods hang over his son's lives, casting shadows as long as lamplight on the roof of a tent. I suddenly realized that the thing I most wanted in life was not to get to know my family better by travelling away from them. I wanted to light their way as clearly as I was able. If that meant, sometimes, travelling with them, like a harassed suburban dad, then that was fine by me.

'Return to your family, frogspawn!' shouted Jack. 'Give up the attempt to survive for ten years in the Arizona desert. We need your credit card!'

I started to climb back up the path.

At the Best Western Inn a mile or so out of the national park, on the road to Flagstaff, there was a swimming pool. There was also a bowling alley and, perhaps more importantly, a bar that served things a little bit stronger than O'Doul's lager. There was a fitness centre, a beauty salon, a jacuzzi, and, so the guide had said, a tennis court. There were at least two restaurants and, so far at any rate, no mention of Navajo fried bread and Hopi stew. There were things like *filet de boeuf en croute*, and roast duckling served in orange sauce, and fine imported wines from places like Bordeaux and the Rhône valley. And, perhaps most important of all, there were two, separate, rooms, both booked in the name of Williams.

I was almost at the top of the path. Ned took off his straw hat. 'Howdey!' he said.

We went on to peer down at other bits of the Canyon. We drove for miles along the road that runs a little south of the rim, and discovered each time we looked into it that it was as wide and ravaged as it had been last time we looked. Even when we got down to the hotel, we were aware of it – with the helicopters clattering jerkily up into the sky, we could sense the thing, waiting for us five miles back up the road. Later on we took a bus out along the west side of the South Rim and watched the sun slip down behind the horizon. It looked like a gigantic crimson penny, and the mountains beneath it looked as if they had been cut out of black paper. Even the company of about seventy-five people, most of whom were filming the sunset and each other (a wizened little Chinaman even loosed off a few close-ups of Harry for good measure) was an impressive sight. But the thing I most remember about the Grand Canyon is walking up out of it after a brief stroll down the stone path that winds down to its floor, and seeing my oldest son grinning at me. I liked the Grand Canyon. As Gavin Simpson had pointed out – it is very, very, very big. But human beings, in my view, are the best type of scenery – especially when they are smiling at you.

9

My night in Las Vegas

From the Grand Canyon to Las Vegas the way lies through the Nevada desert. The next morning we drove back along US 40 towards LA and turned north just past Needles. There was a sign above the road warning drivers not to fall asleep or to drive too close to each other. It's a landscape that could easily cause you to nod off. Glimpsed over the shoulders of John Wayne or Clint Eastwood, it may have a certain charm, but it is not to be taken neat in hundred-mile stretches. A steady queue of cars moved up the highway. Ahead, to our left, was the ominous, grey shape of Clark Mountain, and beyond that the bleak, eroded expanse of the great Nevada basin. When Mark Twain crossed it on his way from the east to Silver City, back in the nineteenth century, the journey he describes in 'Roughing It', they travelled at night and, for large parts of the journey, on foot. We were only sneaking up the southern end of it, but even viewed from an air-conditioned Ford Aerostar, you could begin to understand the awful bleakness of the place for those who crossed it for the first time more than a hundred years ago. The kind of names they use round here – from Death Valley to the Last Chance Motel – make one listen to the engine rather more than usually closely. There are a few isolated houses north of Needles, but as we drifted closer and closer to the eastern border of Nevada, which lay about fifty miles over to our left, the mountains were like the mountains of the moon.

The landscape's only effort at vegetation is a stubby, coarse, green-to-brown growth that may well be what Mark Twain refers to as sage-brush. He got pretty fed up with sage-brush. Although he was a lot closer to it than we were – walking past it, trying to get his pack animals to eat it and lighting it up for fire at night – I could see how sage-brush (if it was sage-brush) could get you down. We went through Grasshopper Junction, declined to turn off to a place called Chloride and pulled up the black mountains towards the Hoover Dam.

The names of the mountains remind you of why Twain and thousands of other Americans came here in the last century. There is Eldorado Canyon, Opal Mountain, Copper Mountain and Micah Peak. They called Nevada the silver state, and millions of pounds worth of the stuff was pulled out of these unforgiving hills. Back down west of Kingman there are the remnants of Calico – a ghost-town. The wooden houses, the wooden bank, the wooden saloon and the mine are all still there, abandoned to the desert the day they ran out of silver.

People come to Nevada now to gamble. In Nevada you can get a drink or lay a bet or pay for sex at any hour of the day or night. When I finally got to Las Vegas, I saw quite a lot of people who looked as if they had been doing all three things continuously for the last five years. Almost the first thing you see as you cross into Nevada on the other side of the Hoover Dam is a giant motel and casino decorated with an electrically-operated board that tells you the odds on craps.

'What are the odds on craps?' said Jack.

'I don't know,' I said; 'I don't even know what craps are.'

Jack snorted contemptuously.

'I don't think we should be going to Las Vegas,' he said, 'if we don't even know basic stuff like that.'

I looked back towards the Hoover Dam – that elegant, colossal slab of concrete wedged into a valley in the black mountains – and chewed my lip.

'We don't have to gamble,' I said. 'We're just going to look at it.'

'What is the point', said Ned, 'of going to Las Vegas if you don't gamble?'

Suzan turned round. 'To watch people gambling!' she said, in a strong, clear voice. 'OK?'

Ned laughed cheerily.

'Watch people gambling?' he said, his voice cracking with amusement. 'Is this a holiday or some kind of aversion therapy?'

85

I said I disapproved of gambling. Harry said he had a confession to make. He said he had played a game called pontoon with a boy called De Kooning. He was not, he said, quite sure of the rules. He had lost a lot of money. He said he still owed De Kooning 25p. We tried to calm him. I said I had had the same experience with a boy called Fromm on a coach between Highgate Junior School and Whitgift in the spring of 1964. There was then quite a lot of lively discussion about the fact that I was alive in 1964. The word 'flares' was mentioned quite a lot, by all three boys. And so, finally, we forgot why we were going to Las Vegas. We drove on through the desert until we came to a town as green as an oasis, where there were lawn-kissing sprinklers on velvet golf courses and acres of newly-built houses with bright yellow walls and tiled roofs in the Spanish manner, of the kind you find in the outer suburbs of London, usually belonging to people who had made their money in rather shady ways.

Boulder City, Nevada, is on the shores of Lake Mead. Since the construction of the 726-foot dam on the Black Canyon, the Colorado river has yielded huge artificial lakes – Lake Mead to the north, Lake Mohave to the south. Lake Mead reaches up north and east as far as the Grand Canyon national park. The leaflet we bought at the Allan Bibles Visitor Centre told us that people flocked to the desert for boating, fishing and water ski-ing, but all we could see as we drove down a dirt road, bleached with sun and laden with dust, was one station wagon parked out on the shore line. When we checked into the motel (AT SEVEN CROWN RESORTS WE CARE) there was an air of desperation about the place. This was not helped by the free copy of the Boulder City bulletin in our room.

'A few years back, when Desert Storm was in full bloom,' (wrote a Boulder City resident), 'Operation Godspeed gave quite a bit of time to encouraging all Boulder City residents to purchase and proudly fly the American flag … '

The reader, signing himself simply *A Patriot*, went on to ask where all the flags had gone. He seemed to think folks in Boulder City were frightened to hang Old Glory out of their front windows. 'This is America, people' he went on. 'There better not be a time when someone tells me I wasn't displaying my country's flag in my community, street or home.'

Funnily enough, I had been going to point out that I had never seen quite so many American flags hung out on poles as in Boulder City, Nevada. There was one outside the gas station, three on the road out to Lake Mead from the town and a particularly ostentatious one outside the golf club. Either *A Patriot* had unusually high standards in the question of stars and stripes display, or else he had been sneaking out late at night and planting them in the front gardens of the slackers of Boulder City, since the date his letter appeared. Suzan said that immediately she got home she would hang a Union Jack out of the front bedroom at 18 Holmbush Road. 'That'll show them,' she said. We were sitting in an air-conditioned room looking out at the volcanic shoreline of Lake Mead. It wasn't only the lake that was artificial. There simply wasn't enough water to make any of the vegetation convincing, and the brave attempt at a leisure industry – the marina, the pool, the car park, the beach – had the abandoned look of something left behind by a space probe. Pretty soon, you felt, the landscape was going to reclaim the gaily-painted blue and white shacks and the flock of boats moored at the jetty on the beach down to our left. After a while I suggested we go down to the marina and take out a boat.

'Why?' said Ned. I was beginning to find his existential approach to the trip exhausting. I started to say that there were a lot of people who would give their eye teeth to take a boat out on Lake Mead. I told him that people were, since the building of the Hoover Dam, flocking to the desert area for boating, swimming, water-skiing and fishing. Ned said he couldn't see them. I said if he wanted dinner he had better come with us. Ned asked what else there was to do in Boulder City. I told him he could always sit and read William Empson's *Seven Types of Ambiguity*. Ned said he had decided that Empson was repetitive, hard to understand and ultimately lacking in coherent purpose. 'Does this mean', I said, 'that you want to come to the marina?' In the end we all went to the marina. Harry said he wanted to jet-ski.

'They won't let you jet-ski,' Jack said, 'you're too small.'

'At what age,' said Harry, 'can you jet-ski?'

Ned laughed lugubriously.

'Thirty-five!' he said. It turned out you had to be eighteen. Harry said he could easily pass for eighteen. We all told him to shut up. He put his baseball cap over to the left, so that the peak stuck out over his left ear. In the end I hired a boat. It was more like a truncated barge than a boat. It had a canopy, a fridge, an outboard motor, a barbecue grill, an emergency flare, five life-saving jackets and it was about twenty foot long and six foot wide. It also had two large portable flags.

'If you decide to swim,' said the man from whom we hired the boat, 'get a representative of your party to wave these flags while you are in the act of swimming.'

I said that I thought that just swimming would be quite exciting enough. He laughed. He had the kind of laugh that is intended to let you know that you've made a joke, even if the recipient doesn't find it funny.

'Boats,' he said in a menacing tone of voice, 'may come and mow you down.'

I could see no boats. There was a man on a jet-ski about a hundred yards out. Otherwise there was just the sun, the blue water and the pale grey hills surrounding it. But the man wasn't finished. He showed me how to drive the thing. He seemed very concerned about what to do when the engine failed. He seemed fairly confident that it would fail. Then the five of us climbed into the boat.

Things were OK as long as we were inside the marina. But as soon as we got out into open water, large waves started to break against the side of the vessel. It didn't take well to this. As the water rose against it, it seemed to rise and go on rising. Even when the waves subsided, it seemed determined to push on up, and when it finally gave up its attempt to shake us over the starboard rail, it fell back heavily onto the lake like a drunk man crashing onto a bed. And then, apparently, completely of its own accord (for I could not see a hidden current or cross-wind that might have made it do so), it started to pitch forwards like an angry horse, and then rear up its prow suddenly as if trying to catch us off our guard and send us, complete with flares and life jackets, flags and fridge, spinning backwards to Lake Mead.

'Go back!' Suzan was yelling. 'You must go back!'

'No!' shouted Ned, 'this is fun!'

He stepped forward to the prow of the boat and started to wave first his left leg and then his right, independently of each other.

'Turn back!' Suzan yelled. 'I don't like boats! Turn back!'

I started to say that if I had known she had a phobia about boats, I would not have shelled out $175 to take one out from Lake Mead marina. She said she had always had a phobia about boats. I asked her once again why she had not told me this before I hired the damn thing.

'I forget,' she wailed, 'until I am actually on one!'

At this point the boat heaved itself up out of the water and started to try and stand on its head. I wrenched the tiller round. I planned to take the boat into the wind. If boats capsized, didn't they usually do so sideways? But if anything this manoeuvre seemed to make the boat even more anxious to be in eight places at once than it had been before.

'We're going to sink!' yelled Suzan. 'Turn back!'

In the end I found about the only spot of Lake Mead that did not seem to be taking the full force of the desert wind. It was about 50 yards offshore from what looked like a sewage outfall. We had a superb view of a particularly dusty stretch of the shore road, and a rather shabby gas station. I turned off the engine and folded my arms.

'We have about three hours and thirty-five minutes to go,' I said. 'Shall we sit it out here?'

I've often noticed that you usually want to return a hire boat long before the end of the time for which you've paid. But this was some kind of record. Ned said he was going to swim.

'Boats will come and mow you down,' said Suzan; 'the man said.' In the end, we came into land with about three hours and fifteen minutes of boating still on the clock. As I wrote out the credit card slip, the glamorous young woman in a wet-suit behind the desk said, 'Yeah. It's too windy for going out there really today.' I didn't bother to ask her why, in that case, she had let me go. I just wanted to leave Boulder City, Nevada. And at 9.30 the next morning, that is exactly what we did.

I find as I get older that my children nearly always know more about any situation in which we find ourselves than I do. I suppose this is all part of the run-up to senility, but as we travelled on towards Las Vegas the next morning, I was often amazed by how quickly information travels between the young – especially information about consumer services.

'When we get to Vegas,' said Ned, 'there is one hotel shaped like a pyramid. And another one called Excalibur where they have a sort of mediaeval castle. A rubber one.'

Harry wanted to know whether it was the sort of castle you could jump up and down on. Jack said he thought it was very unlikely that you would get a *whole* hotel (he put a lot of contempt into the adjective) got up like a *mediaeval castle*.

'What do you mean,' he said, 'they have *arrow slits* and *drawbridges* and a *solar*, and they pour *boiling oil* on you if you leave with your room key … ?'

I was just about to say that I, too, thought it highly unlikely that even Las Vegas would have a hotel got up like a mediaeval castle (it is a good idea in our family to agree with Jack when you possibly can) when we turned the corner and saw a hotel got up like a mediaeval castle. There were even, as far as I could see, a few knights lounging around.

'You see!' said Harry. 'And over there there's one like a lion!' He pointed to the other side of the street. There was indeed a lion about fifty yards away from us. A semi-Cubist lion cast in pale brown, about ten times the size of the pathetic specimens at the foot of Nelson's Column. I found myself looking at something behind it that at first glance looked more like a giant stereo than a building. There was an enormous screen of green windows, a gigantic row of green glass steps rearing up from the strip towards the desert sky, and in front of it two green towers about twice the size of Nelson's Column, on each of which were written the letters MGM.

If the thing was a hotel – and I wasn't at all sure that it was – it had the look of something that had wandered off the lot at Universal Studios. It was big enough to accommodate the entire population of Wimbledon. I looked back across the street at the mediaeval castle. When you looked closely of course it was nothing like a castle. It looked like a huge child's toy. There were about twelve towers, their conical roofs coloured bright red or even brighter blue; none of the towers, all faced in white brick, were built in the same style. They seemed to run the gamut from phoney Siennese to railway station gothic. The one on the far left would have seemed improbable on a cake. At the apex of each cone was something that, at first, I took to be a crucifix, but turned out to be a kind of miniature telegraph pole. On either side of the castle were two L-shaped structures that reminded me of the blocks of flats you see outside Prague, Glasgow or what used to be East Berlin. On each of the four top corners of these twenty- or thirty-storey monstrosities were little bright red or blue caps. Presumably the madman who designed the thing hoped these would help make an easy transition from the Walt Disney fairytale to the Le Corbusier-influenced desire to cram as many punters into the smallest space possible.

Further down the street was a place I discovered later to be called the Luxor. All I could see from here was that it was pyramid-shaped. Perhaps the concierge had the head of a dog, and instead of bathrobes they supplied you with white bandages. I didn't feel like finding out. We had been booked into a place called Caesar's Palace. What was that going to be like? Would we have to speak Latin to the desk clerk?

Before I had time to even imagine what it was we were entering, we found ourselves in a courtyard that stretched back off Las Vegas Boulevard as long as Louis XIV's front garden. Indeed, as we approached it, I was sure we had got the wrong place because, at first sight, Caesar's Palace is pure Louis-Quatorze. There are trim lawns. There are fountains. There is something puzzling and quite alien to Las Vegas about the hotel's facade. It is almost (*almost*) in good taste.

'Where do we park?' said Suzan, as I drifted past a large sign that said VALET PARKING.

'I think', I said, 'they park it for you!' My wife clutched the sides of her seat.

'Where do they take it?' she said. 'Do we get it back?' said Harry. I said I thought we did. Probably. The hotel's front porch is a huge suite of not-uncivilized-looking columns. Behind them – a yellow brick network of buildings that were being fairly honest about the fact that this was a hotel. On the steps where the cars and taxis drew in was a veritable army of men in the kind of jackets I could imagine being worn by the Ruritanian Navy. *People in Las Vegas,* the brochure had said, *usually expect tips.* Did you tip them even when they were not doing anything for you? Should I make the rounds of all twenty or so of them and reward them extravagantly for standing out in the hot sun wearing very foolish costumes? I was strongly tempted to solve this dilemma by driving straight past this line of baggage handlers and car parkers but, instead, I pulled in near the steps and started groping in my pockets for dollars.

A large black face appeared at the window. Suzan started to dig me in the ribs.

'He mustn't see the luggage!' she hissed. I could understand how she felt. I wasn't sure that anyone would be allowed into Caesar's Palace with luggage like ours.

'My knickers are all over the back of the van!' she went on. And she seemed to be getting her head below the level of the dashboard once again. At least, I told myself, this time it wasn't in response to my driving. The man was tapping on the glass. He was friendly but determined. He was, I thought, more like a customs officer than a bell-hop.

'Just gimme the keys!' the man was saying.

As he said this, Suzan jumped out of her seat and, like a squirrel being chased across open country by a dog, dived into the back of the car and began ferreting among the sand-stained canvas bags which contained (among other things) six pairs of boxer shorts, three spare baseball caps, twenty-three pairs of socks, a Fodor's guide to Arizona, four pairs of trainers –

'Let me take these for you!' the large black man was saying.

'Oh no!' Suzan yelped. 'I just need to … ' As the man started to pull cases out of the boot, he revealed what she had been try-ing to hide. Hung along the back seat, like petals on a wet bough, were about three pairs of knickers, four pairs of under-pants and an assortment of socks, drying in the Nevada sun. For a moment I thought the large black man was going to fall on them eagerly and offer to carry them high above his head as he walked before us into Caesar's Palace. Then, tactfully and slow-ly, he averted his eyes. There was no hint of disapproval of our status in his manner. He was just a guy in a canvas jacket with about as much red braid on it as a brothel sofa, who happened to be paid to carry bags. My time on the reservation had altered me. I had to remember that I was a tourist. I had my rights.

'Valet parking?' I heard myself say.

The keys to our car seemed to have been hijacked by a small, swarthy man who was now walking off in the opposite direc-tion.

'Him,' said the large black man.

'Where will he take it?' said Suzan. Suzan said this to me. The large black man gestured over towards the Nevada desert, still visible in the distance, beyond the fringes of this improbable town.

'Over there!' he said.

Then he picked up our baggage and headed off in the same direction. I followed after him a few paces behind, trying to push dollars into his hand. Eventually he stopped, grudgingly accepted a few, and turned once again to his task. This time I let him go.

'Where's he taking them?' Suzan said.

'I don't know,' I said.

'We have nothing,' she said. 'We have no luggage. We have no car. When will they give them back to us?'

'When we've paid them a hell of a lot of money,' said Ned, glumly. Another man, who I couldn't remember having seen before, clutching different bits of our luggage, came in front of us. With the few things left to us we followed him towards the lobby.

Grand hotels are designed to intimidate their customers, and their rituals – like those of prisons or commercial airlines – are there to let you know who is boss. Caesar's Palace continued the naval theme by calling the man who was in charge of taking the luggage up to the room the Bell Captain. I looked back over towards his quarters as I queued to register. A group of the Bell Captain's ratings were standing by, talking to a man in the costume of a Roman Centurion. There did not seem to be any luggage about.

The lobby of Caesar's Palace, like the lobbies of all the hotels in Las Vegas, is shrouded in perpetual night. The light sources were as various as the moods of the Emperor Caligula. There was a boudoir lamp and strip club neon, and by the lifts a brief patch of the heartless warmth that is the standard illumination of the world's hotel. The air was no longer the overheated stuff you had to shovel into your lungs out there on Las Vegas Boulevard. The air conditioning blew it across the dark spaces of the lobby with the control of a barman serving you an iced martini; I found I was sipping it like a cocktail, letting it smack into the back of my nostrils like the first gulp of a joint. And, like marijuana, it slowly changed my perceptions, so that as I came closer to the desk clerk, my thoughts came over the wires of my brain in well-spaced capital letters. The letters were spelling out one question as I trudged back across the huge expanse of carpet that separated me from the dark glass of the lobby front – WHY IS THIS PLACE SO LARGE?

The answer was supplied when I checked us in, and the five of us set off towards the lifts. All this space was not there just for us to stroll through. It wasn't there to create emperor-sized bedrooms, or to give the punter the illusion that he was part of a more gracious age than this. Stretching away to right and left of the path from the reception desk to the lifts was a forest of fruit machines. In front of each machine was a stool, a table on which to place drinks, and also, quite often, a person. Except they didn't look like people. They looked like sculptures by Kienholz, or badly-stuffed guys, or outpatients in a mental hospital who had been so deranged by an endless wait for the right psychiatrist that they had finally lost touch with their own humanity.

94

They were silently yanking silver handles back, and then watching the cards and the apples spin helplessly, waiting for the machines to belch out coins or tokens.

Further on, there were other people, not sitting by machines. They were sitting at green baize tables while attendants dealt out cards to them. None of them were looking at each other, or if their eyes met, it was to exchange the briefest of weary glances, the sort of look you might share with someone when you were about to commit some shameful deed. Everything about these tables seemed to combine the sterility of an operating table with the loneliness of a hotel room.

Each virginal deck of cards was flicked out by bored, immaculate Eurasian girls or portly men dressed in yet another house uniform. I had the impression, as we steered our way between waiters and clients and croupiers and punters, that we had stumbled into a country with laws and a constitution of its own. Each exchange of tokens across the green baize, severely lit from above so that everyone could see what everyone else's hands were doing, was both horribly public and unpleasantly private – like a kiss exchanged under the eyes of a chaperon. It was impossible to tell from anyone's expression whether they were winning or losing. As the card tables were succeeded by roulette tables, and blue or red chips were pushed across onto signs or colours, I half expected some of the lost souls confined to this place at least to let their eyes wander over to the spinning ball on which thousands of their dollars would seem to depend.

But no. Everyone was too weary. Everyone was too busy with the odds to waste energy on a grin or a shout or an unnecessary glance. The only sign of a relationship between croupier and player was at a table where only one man, aged about sixty, in a bright red tuxedo was playing alone. Next to him was a gigantic pile of chips. On his thick fingers were four or five gold, silver and diamond rings, and as he pushed a card back at the dealer, there was something that might have been a smile at the edge of his mouth.

But it was a smile for nobody's benefit but his own. All these lost souls – and I really felt, as we travelled over the vast carpeted spaces of the hotel, that I was walking through the first circle of hell – were quite alone. All of their games were strictly with themselves.

'Are you going to bet?' said Harry.

Suzan seemed mainly preoccupied with what the restaurant had to offer. Ned said he thought we would probably be the only people to have come to Las Vegas to eat.

When we got to the room, a member of Caesar's navy was already there. I hadn't seen him before, but he seemed to have most of our luggage. I was so pleased to see him and it that I offered him $10. He looked at it regretfully.

'Usually,' he said, 'we work out the tip in relation to how many bags I've carried.'

I gave him ten more dollars. There was a silence, then I gave him another ten.

'No,' he said, sadly, 'that is too much.'

'Look,' I said, 'I'll give you my wallet, and you take out what you think you're owed. How about that?'

He laughed then.

'You from England?' he said.

I told him I was. He gave me $7 change.

'I was a miner in Pennsylvania,' he said, 'but here it's better money.'

I said that I was sure it was. The tips alone, I said, must be worth a small fortune. He did not seem in any way touched by the irony implicit in this remark.

'They are,' he said.

Then he told us that a man called Loppnow from Medicine Hall, Illinois or Parker, Michigan, or somewhere miles away from where we were, had just won over $100,000. Were we going to try our luck?

'I am,' I said. 'I'm going to play the roulette tables.'

Suzan gave me a warning look.

When we had got him out of the bedroom, she took me aside and asked me how much money I was going to bet. Harry, who was listening to this conversation, said he wanted $20 because there were good odds on craps.

'I'll stake $10,' I said. 'I have to do it.'

I started to twitch. Ned laughed.

'This we have to see,' he said. 'Nige gambling. We have to see it.'

We stowed the bags away and went down to watch me gambling.

The reality of course was that I didn't know how to gamble. It seemed to me about as difficult as sex had seemed when I was fourteen. I did not know the rules of any of the games I had passed. I was afraid even to approach a fruit machine in case it sneered at me.

'What kind of gambling are you going to do?' said Harry in the lift, as we plummeted downwards.

The big man in the stetson who was sharing it with us grinned.

'The winning kind!' he said.

We laughed. When the man got out, Harry returned to the attack. I told him I would be doing the sort of gambling I was best at. He nodded seriously.

'I may do craps,' I said, 'and I may play poker. Or five-card stud.'

'Five-card stud *is* poker,' said Jack.

Suzan looked at him sharply.

'How do you know that?' she said.

'He knows about gambling,' said Ned, mysteriously. We were at the ground floor. I took out a $10 bill and separated it carefully from all the other bills in my pocket. It was important, I felt, to have the right amount ready.

'I will probably,' I said, as we trooped out into the vast darkness of Caesar's Palace, 'play the wheel.'

'You may win!' said Harry.

No one else seemed to think this was very likely. Clutching my $10 bill I slowed down as I passed the tables. The gamblers were still asking for cards, turning up cards, picking up chips, and laying down chips. As far as I could see, when you wanted to play, you went up to the table and with an amazingly cool flick of the eyes, indicated to the croupier that you were a man among men. The thing to do was to find a friendly-looking croupier. Someone who wouldn't point and laugh when I offered him a $10 bill.

There did not seem to be a friendly-looking croupier around. They all had eyes like boiled sweets, and expressions about as lively as those of your average dead fish. I stopped by one table. A thin young man in a white shirt and a smart black suit was raking in piles of chips. I tried to catch his eye.

'Hi!' I said.

He paid absolutely no attention.

'Why,' said Ned, 'don't you just cram the money into his pocket and run?'

'It's against the rules to give anything to anyone in Las Vegas,' said Jack with a sepulchral laugh.

I went on down past the tables. There seemed to be a conspiracy to ignore me. I got not a flicker from the tiny Chinese woman dealing cards at the blackjack table. The crowded roulette table seemed to be involved in a party all on its own. Even when I got out my $10 bill and waved it and moved from one foot to another, the roulette group just carried on passing $500 chips back and forth across the table. Maybe forty-six-year-old Englishmen in shorts weren't allowed to play. Finally, at a roulette table about thirty yards from the lifts, I decided I had to do something that is not often done at the gaming tables of Las Vegas, Nevada. Speak. I approached the green baize. A fat man in a red dinner jacket looked up at me. I did not run away.

'I would like a chip, please,' I said, firmly.

He didn't react.

'If that is the correct expression,' I went on. 'One of those plastic things, anyway.'

He still didn't respond.

'Ten dollars!' I said. 'Could I have two? If they're in fives, or if you do one dollar ones, could I have ten?' His eyes stirred slowly. He still did not speak. Maybe you had to pay to talk to him. I laughed nervously.

'Or twenty,' I said, 'if you do halves. I could have more than one go!'

There was a sniggering behind me. The three boys and Suzan were standing a few yards away.

'Put it on the red!' hissed Harry.

The man raised his shoulders and lowered his eyes. He seemed annoyed about something. His fat fingers were covered with rings. And none of them, as far as I could see, had any emotional significance. He nodded at the children and jerked his head violently.

'They ... ' he said, 'will have to stand away from the table.'

The State of Nevada (or this particular representative of its gaming community) was clearly worried about the emotional damage liable to be inflicted on young people by the sight of their elders and betters chucking their money away. What I couldn't work out was why such an obscenely pointless transaction should be any less harmful when viewed from a distance of three yards rather than six feet. Did he, perhaps, think that gambling was an infectious disease?

'They just want to watch!' I said.

Jack started to say that he wished to give me advice.

'We have a system!' he said.

Nobody, apart from me, found this funny.

'Move back against the wall!' said the man, in a threatening voice.

Suzan grabbed Jack and Harry.

'Come on, boys,' she said in satirical tones that were as lost as any other form of subtlety in this big, dark, poisonous room, 'Daddy is going to gamble!'

I gave the man my $10. I got one chip back. It was a coloured circular disk. There was no sign on it to tell me how much it was worth. I was quite tempted to dash off with it and carry it back to my room as a souvenir – but, from the expressions around me at the table, it was clear that there was no way but forward.

Something – I forget quite what – had told me that this was a roulette table. I am almost sure that there was a large brass sign saying 'roulette' somewhere. What I was really paying for, though, was a ringside view of the authentic Las Vegas – a square metre of green baize covered with incomprehensible signs. There was no wheel in sight. It was pretty clear that no one was going to help me through the difficult decision regarding Where To Put My Chip.

As far as I could see, some squares or colours were quite empty. Perhaps you were only allowed to put your chips on certain numbers. Perhaps placing a chip on certain signs, colours or numbers would involve you in things far more serious than losing $10. Perhaps enormous bouncers would emerge out of the crowd, tap me on the shoulder, and say – 'Mr Francovetti would like to see you now.' Perhaps the whole table would suddenly burst into shouts of laughter. Perhaps, once I had betrayed the fact that I was probably the only man in the whole of Las Vegas who did not know the rules of any card game apart from beggar-my-neighbour and snap, they would take my chip and solemnly snap it in half in front of the Nevada Commission of Tourism. Perhaps –

Nobody had said 'Faites vos jeux!' There had been no indication that I was supposed to do anything with this $10 plastic circle apart from hold it between my thumb and forefinger. But some of my neighbours were looking pretty busy. I leaned forward and placed it on a white number in the middle of the square. The man next to me raised his eyebrows slightly. I tried to look as if I knew this was an apparently foolish move. At least I hadn't tried to swallow it.

I looked back at my family. Jack held up both thumbs.

'Best of luck!' he said.

The man with the rings was doing something with a pack of cards. I couldn't understand why he wasn't spinning the wheel. He didn't seem to have a wheel. What have cards got to do with roulette? Was I supposed to do something else?

It was only when he started to rake in the chips from the table that I realized I was free to go. And that is exactly what I did. I grabbed Suzan's hand and led the boys at a brisk pace, along row after row of pale-faced worshippers, and the followers of cards and dice and machines, out past the Bell Captain's station and the Roman Centurion (who was still talking to the Bell Captain), out past the eat-as-much-as-you-like carvery, and the complete shopping mall with imitation sky at night, the expensive gift shops, the four fine restaurants and the coffee shop and the huge screen where you can bet on baseball, horses or other forms of physical excellence which you watch from a leather seat in the air-conditioned dark.

We stood there looking across at the street where cars followed each other silently under elevated walkways. We watched a black hooker trade a wad of dollars with a fat man in a black T-shirt. We walked out through the forecourt of the hotel and back down Las Vegas Boulevard. As we turned onto the street, a man in dark glasses tried to thrust a magazine into my left hand. My right hand was clutched tightly around Harry's. I couldn't make out the title of the thing, but the cover seemed to feature a naked girl in leather shorts and no bra, pouting at the camera. I clutched Harry's hand harder. Ahead of me on the left was a huge billboard. On it was a movie image of Phil Collins, about sixty feet high, mouthing the words to one of his songs. He'd be here, the billboard told us, tomorrow night. Other girlie magazines, trodden into the sidewalk, showed images of blonde-haired, naked women, their faces scuffed with the soles of tourists' feet. I looked over to my right, towards the suburban fringes of the city and the big arches of the freeway taking cars away to the Nevada desert. I looked at them for a long time. Although the air felt more like raw human exhaust than anything else, it was better than the air back in Caesar's Palace.

'Gambling's stupid!' said Jack.

'Yes,' I said.

Ned pulled his hat down over his eyes.

'Las Vegas,' he said, 'is OK for one night. But more than one night would be disgusting.'

I put my arms around him. He didn't seem to mind this too much.

'Yes,' I said. 'Yes. I think you got that right.'

10

Life beyond Death Valley

Heading north-west from Las Vegas (or 'Vegas', as this hardened gambler was already learning to call it), the logical way to Yosemite Valley takes you up Highway 95, and then left at a place called Beatty. From there Highway 58 takes you down Daylight Pass to a place called Stove Pipe Wells onto Highway 395, the big lonely road that runs north from above San Bernardino up to Carson City, Nevada and Lake Tahoe. That was where Mark Twain spent a memorable night in the days when there was no one in that part of the Sierra Nevada but him and a few wild geese.

'I don't like the sound of Death Valley,' said Harry. 'Do you die if you go there?'

I said it was only called Death Valley because a few prospectors had got lost there back in the nineteenth century.

'In 1848 or something,' said Jack, who had clearly been reading the same book as me, 'and none of them actually died, did they?'

'Probably not,' I said.

I went on to say that the area had fourteen square miles of sand dunes, 200 square miles of crusty salt flats, 11,000-ft mountains and more than 1,000 species of plants and trees, many of which were unique to the valley – like the blue-flowering Death Valley sage.

'I still don't like the sound of it,' said Harry. 'I don't like the name.'

We were, by now, driving up Highway 95 along something called Rancho Road. The urban strip of Las Vegas had given way to the unchanging browns of the summer desert. To try and divert attention away from our next destination, I asked the company whether they knew that it was illegal to throw away a lighted cigarette in the state of Nevada. They said they didn't.

'What is there to see on this route anyway?' said Jack.

'The Nevada test site,' I said, 'or the Nellis Airport Range. I think they explode small thermo-nuclear devices down here.'

Harry said he thought that driving through a nuclear test site to something called Death Valley was not his idea of fun. He said that he wanted to go back to Universal Studios.

'It's only a name!' I said.

But, by now, I too was getting rather alarmed at the thought of Death Valley.

'We don't *have* to go to Death Valley,' said Suzan. 'It's a holiday. We're not compelled to stagger around the desert with blackened lips, croaking "water, water …"'

I started to slow the car. This seemed to me a very reasonable point. Why should we? We were here to enjoy ourselves, weren't we? Why should we stagger around with blackened lips, croaking 'water, water'?

'Yes,' I said, 'why should we?'

The car halted.

'Let's go back!' said Jack. 'Let's go to Los Angeles.'

'Let's go to Chicago!' said Ned.

'Let's not go to Death Valley!' said Harry. 'Let's go to Oklahoma!'

And so it was that we turned round, drove back down through Las Vegas and went out south-west when we really wanted to go north-west. If they had called it Pleasant Valley, I thought, as we drove down 15 and then turned up 395 towards China Lake and Lone Pine, we would not have had a problem. 395 climbs slowly up the eastern side of the Sierra Nevada, and gradually, as you gain height, the bare desert gives way to fine flat lands in which lurid grass, even in August, was putting in an appearance. It didn't look like fertile country though – more as if someone had sown the vegetation in the hard rock of the High Sierra like a hair implant.

Over to our left were the impassable mountains, the highest of which, Mount Whitney at nearly 15,000 ft, is the highest point of

103

the contiguous United States. The mountains are built of bare stone, a damaged geometry of block on block of treeless granite. From the road they had the look of something in a diorama. As the day darkened and we gathered speed up the two-lane highway, I found myself, as I often did in the desert, hoping nervously for the sign to the next town. The size of this country! The bewildering shifts in climate and geology! The room to do things.

'There's too much of it,' Jack said. 'I'm reading my book.'

The settlements on 395 are often fifty or sixty miles apart which, to an Englishman, often gives rise to the worrying feeling that they won't really be where the signposts say they are. We eventually came, however, to a small town called Lone Pine at about six that evening. There weren't many buildings in town but quite a few of them were motels. In England, a place like this, in the middle of nowhere, would be absorbed by itself. Lone Pine seemed as if its only purpose in life was to wait for strangers to ride through. Perhaps, I thought, as I turned off the engine and climbed out of the car, Americans are so pleased to see each other only because they are frightened by the possibilities of escape the country offers them.

How Americans escape from each other was, although I didn't know it, to be the theme of the next three nights. I couldn't understand, as we strolled down the main street of Lone Pine (which is none other than Highway 395), what one was supposed to *do* with all this wilderness over to our left. You could shoot films in it (I discovered later that the eastern High Sierra doubles as the Wild West in quite a few Hollywood film and TV Westerns, including the Roy Rogers show). You could walk over it (there were quite a number of shops along the main street selling the kind of gear you might find in the English Lake District). Or you could, as we were, stand gawping at it, wondering where you were going for pizza.

The American relationship with landscape can only be understood in the light of their recent history, since they have no other kind. It was not much more than a hundred years ago that the first Americans came from the east across these mountains. It was only in 1851 (not long before my grandmother was born) that they rode into Yosemite Valley and burned the settlement of the resident Indians – the Ahwahnechee. Landscape, for Americans, is still something you travel through to get somewhere else.

'Well,' I heard a woman in the motel say, later that night, 'we were in Pittsburgh. And we thought we would try California.'

Lone Pine still has the look of somewhere hastily assembled the night before last. It doesn't extend more than one row of houses back from the highway – as if to say: 'Go on through! Life is elsewhere!'

And nowhere is the USA's peculiar relationship to its own physical landscape seen so clearly than in its national parks. The next morning we drove west of Highway 395 up the Tioga Pass, and on either side of the road were tall pine trees. The rocks whitened. Jack, whose face was glued to the window, broke off staring at the scenery to remark, 'Did you know that 600 cars went up this road in 1916!' He went on to tell us that Yosemite National Park had been created in 1864 by a bill that slipped through Congress during the Civil War. It hadn't been easy to maintain it. In 1891 the US cavalry had had to ride in to keep people out of the park. Not only that; even after they had established it, people kept grazing their sheep on it, and chopping up the trees and selling them.

'Do you realize,' said Jack, 'that between 1918 and 1930 half a billion feet of timber was lifted from the park?'

Ned said that there seemed still to be quite a lot of it left. In fact, he said, as far as he was concerned we could do with a few less trees in this part of America.

'I mean,' Jack went on, now openly flaunting the guidebook from which he had been reading, 'it's *huge*. The valley floor alone is 2,000,000 square miles.' Ned said the guidebook was obviously full of misprints. But Jack was not to be stopped. In the 1930s, he told us, thousands of people had invaded the place. The State of California had had to use tear gas to get rid of them. It was clearly a place, like so much else in America, where the frontier spirit meant something. And the special quality of

Yosemite is that, unlike say the British National Trust, it is in the paradoxical position of being the guardian of a genuine wilderness. As we pulled up to the top of the Tioga Pass, the trees, the sculptured peaks above us, and the rise and fall of the lower slopes away from the road, seemed to promise what so few places in England can deliver – nature uncontaminated by man. But, just as we were all preparing our minds for still, unravished brides of quietness, and more than a few dozen impulses from woods (vernal), a small fat man in a mountie's hat and a grey linen shirt appeared. He was standing outside a structure that, apart from the fact that it was constructed from folksy timber, bore a close resemblance to the booths that housed NCP car park attendants in the United Kingdom.

'Hi!' he said, 'that'll be $5! $5 a car.'

In return for our money he handed us a leaflet which told you what to do if you saw a bear.

There were quite a lot of other men in hats standing around. There was one further up the road. There seemed to be two loitering among the trees to the left. I'd seen these men before – around the Grand Canyon or in the Painted Desert – but down here they seemed to be better organized. There were two more by the Visitor Centre at Tuolomne Meadows, and as we drove down into Yosemite Valley behind a queue of cars, another one leapt out from behind a tree and started to do the self-important hand signals that are a distinguishing mark of those new to traffic control.

'He's soliciting!' said Ned.

'It's the bears!' said Harry, who was deep in the leaflet that had been given to us as we drove in. 'They're here to protect us from the bears.'

He did not seem happy about the bears. Apparently Bear No. 1,139 had just been shot. It had started to hang around camp sites, and had bashed in the side of someone's camper-van in an attempt to get at their sandwiches.

'Do we have sandwiches?' he said. 'We must finish all our sandwiches. If we have sandwiches.'

I said that Bear No. 1,139 was out of the way, and would bother us no more. Harry said that there was no reason to suspect that Bear No. 1,429, or Bear No. 2,765, were any better. They were probably just cowering back there in the underbrush letting Bear No. 1,139 take all the blame. They would all be at it again soon, he said, no question.

As far as I could make out, the whole leaflet was about bears. What to do when you saw one.

'You clap your hands and shout and jump up and down!' said Jack.

He had obviously been doing research on this subject.

'And also,' said Suzan, who seemed, too, to be remarkably well-informed, 'you remain absolutely *motionless*.' I said I couldn't quite see how you combined both these things. Harry said that as far as he could make out, if a bear smelled so much as a crumb anywhere in your car, he and all the other bears would be over there yanking your rear doors off, poking around in your rucksack.

'We must get rid of all the food and all of the things that smell,' he said, 'and throw them away.'

'What do bears like?' said Suzan. 'Do they like toothpaste?'

There was then a lively discussion about what kind of smell attracted bears. Ned said that they liked the odour of twelve-year-old boys. Baseball caps, he said, really got them going. Baseball caps, he said, were the average bear's idea of a tasty snack. 'Head sandwich!' he said. Harry's face grew very round.

We were now driving down a steep, twisted road past lines of pine trees. Over to our left was a level lake, ringed by the densely architectural peaks of the upper end of the Yosemite Valley. By the lake shore the sandy soil was strewn with pine needles. And by a wooden shack was another of the men in hats. Next to him was a sign that said TO THE GIANT SEQUOIA.

'What's a sequoia?' said Harry. 'Is it a wild animal of some kind?'

I explained that it was a tree. People lost enthusiasm at this news. Ned said that he wasn't getting out of the car to look at a tree.

In fact it wasn't possible for any of us to get out of the car to look at the tree. There was a queue of cars waiting for a chance to see the tree. At the head of the queue was another man in a wide-brimmed hat. I backed the car out into the road, and we travelled on down the hill.

The Tioga Pass road joins Highway 120, from the west, at the edge of the Stanislaus National Forest. It was only when we turned left back up the valley that we saw the famous, much-reproduced view of Yosemite. As we got closer to the camp ground on the upper part of the valley floor the Half Dome, the huge, pure white slab of granite rock, reared up over the pine trees. Forests, especially pine forests, have a way of smothering the contours of the place. From above, they can resemble nothing so much as a wall-to-wall carpet and, from inside, they have all the charm of an airy, resinated cupboard. But in Yosemite the rocks are at war with the trees; they break out of the forest in spires and squares and domes like modernist cathedrals. For a moment I could understand why John Muir, the Scots naturalist, had worked so hard to keep this view the way it was.

Then another man in a hat sprang out from the trees and started waving his arms. Over to our left, through a screen of pines, I saw a row of cabins and, beyond it, a river. Two youths with backpacks and baseball hats – both caps switched so that the peak jutted out behind – came towards us on the other side of the road. Suddenly a coach pulled round the corner. On its front were printed the words THE HAPPY ISLES.

'My God,' said Suzan, 'this is … '

'Appalling?' said Ned.

I do not think I have ever seen a landscape so quick to change from the awesome to the banal as at Yosemite. The valley floor has been desecrated by something far worse than sawmills, Indians or sheep. It has been handed over, entire, to the men in wide-brimmed hats. And the park rangers have put up notice-boards telling you where you are, log cabins, tent cabins, swimming pools, restaurants with ridiculous Indian names, bearproof bins, visitor centres, backpacking stores, cycle paths, footpaths and one-way streets.

All of the architecture of the Yosemite Valley screams quietly at the visitor: I'M NOT REALLY HERE! DON'T MIND ME! It is constituted on the entirely fallacious principal that it is possible to design a hamburger bar that blends easily with the landscape of the surrounding terrain.

The thing is, Yosemite does not belong to the bears or the ground squirrels or the rattlers, or even the backpackers. It belongs to the rangers. Just when you think you have finally got away from it all – when you're toiling up the John Muir trail towards the Half Dome or taking a round trip up Cascade Creek – out of the undergrowth comes a ranger to tell you that there is marshy ground ahead, and they have just had to lift three people off by helicopter.

Curry Village is a sort of shanty town of wood and canvas cabins set on the soft, sandy ground just off one of the busiest car parks I have ever come across in the wilderness.

'Presumably,' said Harry, 'the bears stay away from the actual village.'

Ned (who had now got hold of the pamphlet) said that, as far as he could make out, they were all headed in this direction. There were also, he said, mountain lions. There was, apparently, a whole section on what to do if you met a mountain lion.

'What do you do?' said Harry.

I parked the car amongst some trees, and Suzan set about removing all organic material from the interior.

'Grab a stick,' said Ned, 'apparently. Oh, and *if attacked, bite back!*'

Harry gulped. Suzan was whirling things out from the back of the car. Bottles of fruit juice, a mouldy piece of cheese, some fragments of hamburger, and several half-eaten packets of what Harry was now calling potato chips.

'Where do we put them?' said Harry. 'Do we have to bury them?'

'We must throw away all organic material,' said Suzan.

'Including ourselves!' said Jack.

Suzan did not smile.

'Unless we have a bear-proof canister!' she said. 'Did anyone think to bring a bear-proof canister? Or is that another thing that I am supposed to have done for this family?'

I said no one expected her to have brought a bear-proof canister. As far as I was concerned, I was quite happy to lose some mouldy old cheese, and a few rotten crisps.

'And the toothpaste,' said Harry. 'They might eat the toothpaste.'

'Give it to them,' I said. 'Put it out for them. Give them a brush while you're at it. And some shower gel!'

Yosemite was getting to me. I didn't feel as if I was in the middle of the remote High Sierra. I felt the way I had done when the five of us drove our hired camper-van into another dismal, rain-sodden Scottish camp site.

I carried the suitcases over to our three tent cabins. In each one were two metal beds of the kind found in dormitories at English public schools. There were blankets that looked as if they had come from the same place. I sat on one of the beds. After a while Suzan came in.

'They're very worried about the bears,' she said. 'We shouldn't have told them about the bears.'

'You can hardly avoid hearing about the bears,' I said. 'There are notices about them everywhere. There are videos telling you how to behave on every street corner.'

Jack appeared in the doorway of the tent cabin. He was wearing a loose-fitting T-shirt, track suit bottoms and a baseball hat. He looked, as he has done since the day he was born, moderately pleased to be here.

'They have something called a wilderness permit,' he said. 'If you want to go into the back country, you get a permit.'

Harry appeared next to him. Jack snorted to himself.

'Presumably one of those men in hats goes with you,' he said.

I turned my face to the canvas wall of the tent.

'I vant to be alone,' I said.

I don't think I have ever felt less alone than in the four days I spent in the Yosemite Valley. I have never had such an intense, close-up view of quite so many different Americans. There was the fat man in shorts who videoed the dinner menu at the village grill in Yosemite village. There was the thin black man who had, he told me, waited one hour and forty-five minutes to be served at the Terrace Pizza, Curry Village. There was the enormous blue backside I followed all the way up the mist trail to the top of the Nevada Falls. It belonged to a woman who told me she lived in a 'not very nice area of Los Angeles'. There was the man in the tent next door who, every morning at 9.30, speaking only slightly more slowly than President Reagan, outlined what he and his family were going to do the next day. There was the driver of the free Yosemite shuttle bus who, on a journey from the upper camp grounds to the housekeeping camp, instructed us all to lean out of the glassless windows and shout 'Hello, bears!'

Americans are like other people, only more so. Americans on holiday are even more like Americans than usual. Had I been a sociologist anxious to write an account of the American family, or the marketing research manager of a fast-food chain, I could not have come to a better place. But, as the days wore on, I began to get very anxious to leave the huge white slab of rock above us, the Merced River winding its way to the camp grounds, and the pine woods that echoed, night and day, to the sound of Mom and Dad being reasonable.

Jack and Harry, too, were becoming unhealthily obsessed with bears. They were frightened to go to the lavatory after dark. I, too, was frightened to go to the lavatory after dark, largely because, whenever I did, I seemed to find the same gigantic black man shaving at the wash basin. But the boys were frightened of bears. They said they were pretty sure they had seen one hanging around the lavatories. They said it was obviously waiting for the opportunity to nip in and start guzzling the toothpaste. When I suggested a hike into back country, they looked at me curiously.

'You must be *mad*,' they said; 'it is *stiff* with bears. What are you trying to do to us? It's bad enough that we have to spend the night in a cabin with a canvas wall, but –'

I took them to the Visitor Centre where more men, not all of them in hats, were selling maps of Yosemite, videos of the Yosemite experience, Yosemite scarves and Yosemite histories. I showed them the map on the wall which gives the numbers of bear–human encounters for the previous year. I explained that, when you considered the thousands of people who visited the park every year, there were remarkably few encounters.

They were not convinced. Harry gazed past me at a small printed card that read:

BUY A BEAR-RESISTANT FOOD CANISTER.
IN AN EFFORT TO DECREASE INCIDENTS BETWEEN
BEARS AND PEOPLE …

Jack read this several times.

'You see,' he said, 'incidents. There are incidents between bears and people.'

I pointed out that incidents didn't necessarily mean people being eaten. Maybe the bears had just tried to get hold of their sandwiches. Maybe they had sat up on their hind legs and done tricks for them. Jack said that incidents meant that bears had more or less thrown their weight about.

'We have to pee in the waste-paper basket,' he hissed. 'It's unbearable. Yesterday morning Harry had to sneak it out in case one of the rangers found it.'

It turned out that the two of them had been on their way to the Gents' with a wastepaper basket full of pee when they had seen a ranger looking at them oddly. They had fled into the bushes, where, about fifty yards from the cabin, they had found a bear-proof dustbin into which they had tipped the circular steel container (property of the American National Parks Service) almost full to the brim with British urine. They had spent the next day waiting for someone from Yosemite Refuse Disposal to instigate a camp-wide search, complete with compulsory fingerprint and urine analysis.

We seemed to spend most of our time trying to find a decent restaurant. Since Suzan had thrown away all the food in the car, and since everyone agreed that it was dangerous to even mention the word food in the vicinity of our tent cabins, we checked into Indian Lodge, the Ahwahnee Grill, the Loft, Degnans Delicatessen, and various other establishments in which big-boned, happy-looking American women asked if we had had a nice day, and whether we would like soup or salad. The only bit of nature any of my children seemed to explore closely in the Yosemite National Park was thousand-island dressing.

'Tomorrow,' I would say, gazing out of the window of wherever we happened to be eating, 'we're going on a hike. We're going up the Half Dome.'

I spent quite a lot of time looking at maps of the Half Dome. I looked at quite a few pictures of the famous tables sunk into the rock on the last 'terrifying' section of the climb. I wondered, aloud, how we would all cope with the tables. I read several descriptions of the paths up to the Half Dome. I sometimes read them, aloud, at the dinner table.

'When we're up there,' I would say, 'the views will be terrific.'

'When *you're* up there,' Jack would return, as he lowered his face into his clam chowder.

'It's a thirteen-hour round trip,' I would add, 'so it's up with the lark!'

But somehow or other I always woke up just too late. I would come to at about four in the morning and start to think, 'Two hours to go.' I would lie alone in the dark, thinking about those tables and how I would have to lead everyone off the mountain if there was the least sign of thunder. I would calculate exactly how much water we might need to carry to avoid dehydration, and wonder why I had forgotten to buy a bear-proof container in which to put our sandwiches. Not that I had made any sandwiches. Or, for that matter, had anything to make sandwiches with. Or …

But, by the time I had finished thinking about all these things, I had slipped back into peaceful sleep, and suddenly it was 10.30 in the morning, and Curry Village was full of trainee park rangers wheeling huge baskets of laundry.

On our last day, I persuaded them to walk the seven miles up to the Nevada Falls. I didn't, of course, tell them it was seven miles.

'Shall we just … go a little … further up the path … ?'

As they walked, they seemed to lose their fear of incidents between bears and people. But there were so many people, the only kind of bear–human incident was liable to be a bear crushed to death in the stampede.

'Oh look!' said Harry. We were toiling up the mist trail, a steep track by the Merced River where it tumbles over a curtain of rock, which breaks the river's descent from Merced Lake at about 1,900 ft.

'Look! There's the man we saw in the Mountain Room Broiler with a handkerchief on his head!'

He was quite right. As I looked around I could recognize in the line of people struggling up the rocks, some of them damp from the river spray, quite a few of my fellow campers. I was almost sure that the dour-looking man in glasses going up the trail about a hundred yards ahead of me was the man in the queue for the laundromat at Housekeeping Village. And weren't those three youths in baseball hats the ones who had been asked to leave the Yosemite Valley free shuttle bus by a rather querulous female ranger? On that occasion, I recalled, the man next to me had revealed that he, too, was a ranger.

'Not all of us,' he told me darkly, 'wear uniform.'

As we came up to the waterfall, I wondered how many undercover rangers there were. Presumably some of them deliberately infiltrated groups with wilderness permits and tempted them into indiscretions somewhere up there in the lonely hills north of the Half Dome. I could picture the scene all too well.

'Shall we just … light a camp fire, without using established rings?' says the undercover ranger.

'Well … ' say his fellow backpackers, 'I'm not sure … '

'Go on,' he hisses, 'no one will know … '

The hiker stoops to comply and, before he has time to recant, he is clapped in irons and taken off to the Visitor Centre, to be re-educated in the John Muir sensory deprivation chamber.

The Mist Trail goes into the rock for the last few yards – a narrow passage, with a rail on one side, cut into the granite. At my left was the brilliant white spray of the falls, catching the light as it fell and spawning rainbows to dazzle the astonished tourists. Up at the head of the falls is a huge slab of near-level rock worn as smooth as a dance floor, and at the far end of it the Merced, translucent brown, flows calmly into the knife-edge of the granite; from the upper falls there is no hint of the wildness of the spray beyond it, as the river swings out like a swallow-diver and falls hundreds of feet to the rocks below.

After a while the five of us went on up the side of the river. Most of the other tourists had taken different tracks now, or turned back down the steep path to the valley, and, as we pushed further up the hill under a wooden bridge, the noises of humanity grew fainter and fainter. On a long stretch of smooth stone about thirty yards up from the falls, some children were sliding down the rock into one of the river's deep pools, shaded by trees. And then, as we picked our way through the rocks, there was just us and the clear water of the river. You could follow this, I thought, all the way up to the source. You wouldn't need wilderness permits, you would just walk and stop and skim stones, the way I did when I was a kid in Wales or the Lake District with my brothers. You get further and further away from Degnans Delicatessen and the Awani Lodge Hotel and the half-hour performance of the spirit of John Muir at the Yosemite village Visitor Centre. At night, high up here, away from the valley floor, the silence would be endless. There would be no noise but the water falling through space or flowing over gravel or swirling and lapping in deep, shaded pools.

We sat by the river and rested after our climb.

'This,' I said, 'is what we came for.'

'It's nice,' said Ned, nodding thoughtfully. No one was reading or listening to tapes or arguing. Harry was lying on his back, staring up through the trees at the dappled light. Suzan was staring into the clear water, lost in thoughts that, even after more than twenty years together, I do not hope or seek to catch or control.

'Nature,' I said. 'That's what Yosemite's all about.'

At this point a man stepped out of the trees behind us. He was wearing a gigantic grey hat, a dark green uniform cut from military-looking thick cloth. He was wearing a badge and, on his left hip, a revolver. He was pale and overweight, and he looked as if something was paining him.

'Sir,' he said, 'I am a park ranger.' We gawped at him. What did he think we thought he was? Perhaps he imagined we would assume he had just wandered off from some Nazi rally.

'I am reminding you,' he went on, 'for your own safety and protection, that you may not bathe in the river. Or, at least, that is what I would recommend for you at this time.'

No one reacted. He smiled nervously and continued to speak as if reading from a prepared statement.

'Last week,' he went on, 'three people were lifted out of here by helicopter. I am simply informing you all of this situation, and hope you have a nice day in Yosemite Valley National Park.'

I looked up at him.

'Thanks,' I said.

'Don't want to spoil the fun,' he said. 'You all have a good time!'

'It's OK,' I said, 'we were just leaving anyway.'

We got up and walked back down the river to join the people. I thought again about the Hopi Indians. If we – the white man – wanted to discover why we had come to this beautiful place, how we got control of it, and what it was able to teach us now, I wondered if any of our accounts could match theirs. Yosemite has turned the white man towards caution, geology, discipline, and a certain dogged wonder, but there is no poetry there. And precious little of unreformed nature. It belongs to the eighteenth century rather than the nineteenth. But its rocks and stones and trees and rivers tell a story that the Hopi would know only too well. A story in which the white man gains control over the wild places of the world and knocks their spirits into shapes that resemble his own.

11

Gold and wine and flowers and mud

North-west of Yosemite lie the foothills of the Sierra Nevada. It's a rolling landscape of the kind of understated hills you might find in England or rural France. As we drove through it on Highway 49, even in early August, with the grass burnt brown by the sun, it suggested things I hadn't thought existed so near Los Angeles – wild flowers, vines, olive trees and well-stocked gardens. The villages crowded up the narrow road as anxious to please as their counterparts in rural Gloucestershire. The houses were of wood, their picket fences shining white. There were wooden churches, too, square and decent, their triangular spires showing the traveller the domestic way to Jesus.

The road started to do something very un-American, too. It started to twist and wind between the whitening fields. Towns no longer started as a stain on the horizon, hung there as you gobbled up the miles, and then were gone in a thunderstroke, like a railway platform abandoned by a through express; they came upon you, cutely, around motherly corners. Sometimes they were shy enough even to have taken themselves away from the highway, and when I turned off the road into Jamestown, one of the first towns by-passed by the highway, the first word I thought of was 'home'.

There were buildings that looked like Shaker barns and turned out to be banks. There were folksy wooden houses that seemed to suggest that they were the birthplace of some nine-teenth-century lady poet, and turned out to be electrical shops. There were wooden sidewalks and front porches in brilliant white, eggshell blue or crimson red. The main street looked as if someone had been out there on their hands and knees with a mop and bucket since six o'clock that morning.

'It looks,' said Jack, 'like a set of kitchen units.'

'I like it,' said Ned; 'in fact – I think it is the nicest place I've seen in America. So far.'

It is, of course, absurd even to dream that you know what is going on in the minds of your children. I wondered at first whether his remark might not be some subtle form of criticism of the whole trip. Surely he couldn't really imagine that a few coloured houses, a selection of window boxes and the odd neo-colonial verandah amounted to anything special. Or was he just responding to the fact that, at long last, there was seabass on all the restaurant menus? Was it simply that the place reminded him of Wimbledon?

'There are antique shops!' said Suzan.

I tried to look pleased about this. I don't think I succeeded. I didn't imagine that I would ever feel nostalgic for Yosemite. But at least it was low on antique shops. Suzan had that animated, furtive look she gets near antique shops. I have got, over the years, better at dealing with this harmless obsession of hers. I can even ask with some semblance of courtesy, after she has been in one –

'How was it?', or 'How was it for you?'

But on this occasion my face betrayed me. She lowered her head and scuttled towards the antique shop. From the front it looked like a dolls' house. So much so that I was expecting at any moment a huge hand to come out of the sky, pick Suzan up by the scruff of her neck, and slip her into it through a first-floor window. I thought about the amazing power of antique shops. How they are always uniquely themselves. They evoke exactly the same emotions in me whether they are located in James-town, California or the Ridgeway, Wimbledon. It is not exactly despair, but it is close to despair. It is like sadness, but it is not sadness. It is a sort of dull ache. Later, in Mystic Seaport, Connecticut, she forced her way into the Christmas Shop. It was packed, even though it was still only August 12th. I didn't go in, but she told me later there was a long seat by the door labelled HUSBANDS' BENCH. There was no sign of any such facility in the main street of Jamestown, California.

'Perhaps,' said Ned, 'there will be a guitar shop or something.'

'She'll be *ages*,' said Harry.

Jack thrust his hands deep into his tracksuit trousers and kicked the pavement, hard.

'Antiques!' he said with savage contempt.

We walked up the main street looking for a guitar shop. There didn't seem to be one. There were, however, three or four more antique shops. Even the shops that weren't antique shops looked worryingly like the sort of shops Suzan likes.

'When she comes out,' Ned said, 'don't hang around. Let's slip a bag over her head and force her into the back of the van before she sees any of them.'

'She's seen them,' said Jack, sitting on a low wall and putting his head into his hands. 'It's too late.'

We stood by the door of the shop. Then, although it went against the grain, we peered around the edge of it to see if we could see her. She was in the far corner with her head well down.

'If she sees any of us,' said Jack, 'yawn and look at your watch.'

'She won't look up,' I said. 'She knows better than to look up.'

Ned said we should go in there and get her out. We should just walk in there, go up to her, tap her on the shoulder and request her, firmly but politely, to leave. We laughed pityingly at this suggestion. I think we all knew, deep down, that to go into the shop was to admit defeat. If we went into the shop and approached her, I told them, she would go on the attack. She would hold up a wooden doll or an eighteenth-century commode and say –

'What do you think of this?'

She would thrust it into our hands then and, before we could think of a decent response, scurry off to another part of the shop. 'She knows what she is doing,' I said.

'I could pretend to be in pain!' said Harry.

'That won't stop her,' said Jack, miserably. 'Pain is nothing when you're looking at *antiques* … '

I can't remember how we eventually got her out. Or whether

she did carry a little bit of Jamestown's past into the Ford Aerostar van. But I do know that from there until we got to Sacramento, history became an awkward, intractable theme for all of us. Sonora, the next town up the highway, has the second-oldest frame church in California. It was built in 1860, twelve years after James Marshall found a nugget of gold in the stream near a sawmill he was building on the American river. All these neat wooden towns, from here up to Nevada City, about a hundred miles north, were built during the gold rush which swelled the population of California from 15,000 to 265,000 in only three years.

Now, most of the gold has gone (they had taken out 750,000,000 tonnes of gold by 1865), and the towns seemed to make most of their money from tourism. They have plunged into re-enacting their past with all the enthusiasm of prospectors. Just outside Sonora is a small town called Columbia. It was founded in 1850 and is now a theme park, a model version of a town of the 1850s, in which you can take a ride in a real Wells-Fargo stagecoach, watch documentary films about the mother-lode, the stretch of gold that runs up the valley right to Nevada City – and watch a blacksmith at work in a real 1850s forge.

Except, of course, it is not a real 1850s forge. The only buildings that date from anywhere near the 1850s are the Presbyterian church and the schoolhouse. There are quite a lot of people in nineteenth-century costume. They are in the Wells-Fargo express office, running a non-existent newspaper, and in the store that sells gold-diggers T-shirts, CDs of authentic mining songs and hats that tell everyone you meet that you have been to Columbia State Historic Park. The man selling tickets for the stagecoach in the Wells-Fargo office was wearing a green eye-shade and an Edwardian suit, but the way in which he turned to his assistant as he passed over my 'ride shotgun' pass when we stepped up into the coach was pure 1990s.

'How much have we done today?' he said.

'150,' said his friend.

'That's bad!' he replied, and then switched back into being someone from the 1850s, by resting his chin on his hand and allowing his eyes to glaze over. Theme parks, like well-stocked gardens and antique shops, are familiar territory to me. There are times when I think the whole of England is nothing but a theme park. Perhaps in some far-off time our descendants will be re-creating our present in the same spirit. Perhaps years from now somebody will pay money to 'hire' a car from a man got up to look like a genuine employee of Hertz from the last decade of the second millennium. Perhaps whole families will pay even more to eat a genuine 'hamburger with cheese' served to them by a youth in an authentic 'baseball hat'. But I always find historic theme parks quite alarmingly post-modern. They ask so many completely unanswerable questions about what the past is. They are so clearly about endowing places and people with atmospheres and feelings that are wholly alien to them. They are re-enactments of rituals common to now and then, or often re-definitions of the past in terms of the present. They remind me, for some reason, of those 700-page books that have a rhinoceros, a rabbit or a bank vole as the hero.

'Next,' Jack said, as we went into the Columbia City Hotel (1856) for 'spring greens with cherry tomatoes and caramelized walnuts in cassis hazelnut vinaigrette', followed by 'seabass in two olive crusts and provençal gratin', 'they'll have an Anglo-Saxon theme park on Wimbledon Common. You'll be able to have Anglo-Saxon breakfast and watch real Anglo-Saxon churls chuck woad at each other!'

'Don't say it too loud,' said Ned. 'You may give these guys ideas.'

Later, Harry panned for gold. This involved rinsing muddy water through a sieve. They had, apparently, put gold in the mud, but Harry couldn't find it. He maintained, afterwards, that the small Japanese boy next to him had pinched his gold. I thought this was probably the most authentic prospector-like moment of the entire day.

Finally we went on the stagecoach. It was – somewhat to my surprise – a real stagecoach. It was uncomfortable enough to be genuinely authentic. We swayed off into a patch of waste ground. A masked man on a horse rode up and asked us if we had any gold. We said we hadn't. Then he waved his revolver at Ned and asked him what he could do for a poor outlaw who had lost his claim. Ned said he would be prepared to sing 'We Wish You a Merry Christmas!' The man said that was fine. Ned sang. Then we jolted back to the Wells-Fargo office.

'It was an actor!' said Harry. 'That man in a mask who said he had lost his gold. It was an actor!'

A lot of people made a lot of money out of the gold rush. Even Mark Twain was a millionaire for a day. But, like most humorists, he had little luck. He was – as I have been most of my life – a little too late with the paperwork. Someone else got his claim. Near Columbia in Calaveras County there is a place that gave him the idea for the story that made his name. The tale is about a man who weighted down a jumping frog with lead shot in order to spike its chances, and for reasons not clear to me, or to Twain, it made him suddenly famous. But when you read Twain's account of the immigrant towns, you start to understand this part of America in a way no amount of sepia photographs, banjo playing juke-boxes or men in waistcoats pretending to be nineteenth-century waiters could ever do. It was quite clearly a haphazard time. No one in the hills of California had any history. Everyone was passing through. The people who have stayed, like the Sacramento millionaire Samuel Brannan, are those in the service industry. In the long run it may be more profitable to persuade people to pretend to pan for gold than it is to actually haul the stuff out of the ground. Perhaps tourism is the activity predicted by Keynes in the General Theory, when he recommends governments to set their unemployed workers digging holes in the ground, building monuments, doing anything in order to keep the wheels of the economy turning. What the Columbia State Historic Park tells us, I decided, as we drove back into Senora, was nothing to do with the 1860s. It had a lot to say to the 1990s. Everything is shadow boxing now, it said, everything has been discovered. When the millennium comes, it won't be a bang or a whimper, it'll be some guy coming up to you at your table and whispering softly in your ear: 'The bill, sir'. He will say it very, very softly because he will know that neither you nor anyone else has any hope of paying.

When we turned off Highway 49 towards Sacramento, the country flattened out. There were huge fields on either side of the road, a four-lane highway, and everywhere there were flowers. There were flowers being grown in regiments behind tall, wire fences. There were flowers piled high on lorries, rumbling up the highway. There were flowers in the quiet gardens of the city's houses.

'This is the original capital of California,' I said to the troops.

Suzan was more preoccupied with finding a way out of it.

'Where are we going now?' said Harry.

'We are going,' said Suzan, 'to wine country. When we can find the fucking freeway.'

Harry's eyes grew wider. I could see him trying to imagine what was meant by wine country. Perhaps he pictured it as a gigantic off-licence somewhere in the dry, barren hills. Perhaps he thought it was an alcoholic version of the Big Rock Candy Mountain. As we drove down the wide freeway towards San Francisco, I tried to imagine it.

All famous places are inevitably disappointing, but none so much, perhaps, as the homes of famous wines. I can still remember the puzzled sense of loss I experienced as I discovered that Saumur looked a bit like Finchley. Chablis wasn't a lot better. I don't know whether there is actually a place called Muscadet, but I imagine it as a dreary suburb of some town in the Loire, with the grapes huddled together behind a hypermarket.

The Napa Valley, however, lives up to the promises it made to me from the first shelf on the right at Oddbins, Wimbledon – a place I visit almost as frequently as your average nun does her nearest altar. It starts as a rather drab turn-off from the freeway into San Francisco. Where, you think, as you come over the hill and see a gas station, a roundabout, and a queue of cars, is the valley? It's not until you leave the town of Napa behind, travelling north-west along Highway 29, that the Sonora mountains take shape on your left, and the road climbs next to the Napa river, past Robert Mondavi's huge Italianate mansion, fronted by acres of luminous green vines ranged at attention under the

123

brilliant sky. Vineyards to me always suggest wrinkled old women in black skirts and scarves, ageing stone warmed by the sun, and the worn faces of a peasant population half as old as the hills. The Californian vineyards are not like that. There is nothing gnarled in the Napa Valley apart from the branches of the vines, and even they look as if they've all been recently rubbed down with furniture polish. Everyone is young and clean and tanned and optimistic. It seems impossible to believe that any of them drink the stuff they produce. The nearest thing to a red-nosed wreck, as we drove up through the valley, was me. I was anxious to get as much free booze down me as I possibly could in the time available. I looked longingly up at the wineries as we passed spacious buildings set well back from the road, built, for the most part, in the up-to-the-minute mediaeval style you find in a certain kind of English supermarket – Sainsbury's quattrocentro. Inside there, I kept thinking, are thousands and thousands of bottles of Chardonnay – Phelps, Stagsleap, Glen Ellen, Gisborne (or was that from Australia?), gallon upon gallon of buttercup yellow stuff that, taken in sufficient quantities, can make you rise above the world's indifference. Nobody else wanted to stop.

'Why don't you just go into a shop and buy a bottle and gulp it down and be sick, like normal people!' said Ned.

I pointed out that I was not Michael Uzbicki of Southfields or Jeremy Algar of Raynes Park or any of the other seventeen-year-old louts from King's College School who had been sick all over my back lawn during the past nine months.

'Uzbicki wasn't sick,' said Ned, 'he just looked a bit green. Algar was sick, I grant you. Howlett was sick. Victor Chung was sick. Twice. But Uzbicki never actually vomited. He retched.'

'He retched,' I said, gripping the steering wheel tight, 'dangerously close to my shoes.'

This seemed to amuse Ned. I said that for me wine was something more serious. I liked to taste it, I said, to roll it around my tongue and experience the creamy complicity of Chardonnay and the ironic tang of Sauvignon.

'And then be sick, like everyone else!' said Ned.

Jack said that he thought it was impossible to talk about wine without being pretentious.

'Suppose I said a McDonalds cheeseburger had a full-bodied nose, or a McChicken sandwich had a forthright quality redolent of cardboard!' he said.

I said that I would say that was a fairly good description of a McChicken sandwich. Ned said how could I know since I've never eaten one. I spent my time stuffing my face in new-wave Italian restaurants. We hadn't come 4,000 miles so that I could swill a few bottles of Chardonnay and fork bucketfuls of polenta down my gob. Suzan said that was exactly why we had come 4,000 miles. Waving a copy of a book called 'Access to Wine Country', she said that for once in a while we were going to do what the grown-ups wanted to do. She had found a three-star restaurant, and we were going to shove our faces with a lot more than polenta, and they were going to shut up and enjoy it. Harry said he hated polenta and he hated wine. He also said a boy in his class had recently drunk half a bottle of vodka at a party. Suzan demanded to know the name of the boy. Harry said he couldn't remember. Ned said he was making it up as usual. And so, arguing, sneering, re-cycling old jokes and amusing each other if nobody else, the Williams family came into Calistoga Town at the head of the Napa Valley.

Calistoga was founded by that Sacramento millionaire Sam Brannan, and its name, so they say, is the result of a verbal flip he made when announcing the foundation of the resort at a banquet. Brannan meant to say that he was going to found the Saratoga of the West, but the word came out as Calistoga. The place itself looks almost uncannily deliberate. The brightly-painted wooden shop fronts, set back from those unnaturally wide American streets, once again concealed restaurants, art galleries, craft shops and other things that quickly reduced Ned, Jack and Harry Williams to speechless apathy.

'You must have a mud bath!' Suzan said. 'They do mud baths here, and there are hot springs!'

This didn't seem to go down much better.

We cruised the streets until we came to a long, low, white

building, flanked by stucco cottages; over to its left was another façade at the head of a winding white staircase that looked as if it was waiting for somebody famous to walk down it. A notice on the door said this was Indian Springs, founded by the millionaire Sam Brannan. A woman inside, in the sort of outfit worn by the receptionist of an expensive private lunatic asylum, said we could have a facial at four o'clock. Ned said he didn't want a facial at four o'clock. Jack said, in quite a loud voice, that he would like hand relief at half-past-three or else there would be trouble. Somehow or other we got the lads out of there.

But Suzan was determined to get at least one of us into a mud bath.

'It's volcanic ash!' she said; 'it's good for you! Come on!'

Down the street, Dr Wilkinson, an apple-cheeked man of pensionable age, in a short-sleeved white shirt and a smile calculated to take the heat out of any bill, was offering the Dr Wilkinson facial, a multi-layered facial that included cleansing, gentle scrub, facial mineral steam, deep cleansing hand and foot moisture massage with heated mittens and booties, facial massage, mud mask and mousse. We could have that, said the young woman behind the desk, now. It only took an hour and a half. We looked up at the picture of 'Doc' Wilkinson. Next to it, it said THE MAN THE MUD AND THE MAGIC. Behind the elegant young woman at the desk was an even more elegant young man. He was talking to someone on the phone, his wrists snaking in the cool, air-conditioned air like a Javanese dancer. He leant forward. We could have a salon facial, an executive facial, a minifacial, an acupressure face lift, a salt-glow scrub, or an earth and sea body treatment. Did we want that? Jack thrust his face forward.

'We'll have five executive facials,' he said, 'and we're in a hurry!' Suzan glared at him. She said we wanted a mud bath. She said this in tones that suggested that we all wanted to take one together.

'Right down the street,' said the young man with obvious relief. 'This is not the mud bath department. This is the beauty salon.'

'He must have thought we were a bunch of poofs!' said Ned as we went out into the baking daylight of the Napa Valley.

'You are a bunch of poofs!' said Suzan. 'And you all need a bloody facial.'

Harry, who seemed overawed by all this, was muttering that no one had better try and give him an executive facial. Or touch his penis. He said he thought these places were full of people trying to touch your penis. Ned told him no one was interested in his penis. Harry said, darkly, that quite a few people were, actually.

The five of us went into the mud bath department – a cool, tastefully furnished room, smelling of soaps and lotions. There were wickerwork chairs, trays of soft drinks and, once again, the atmosphere of a rather sinister private hospital.

'Mud baths!' said Suzan to the attendant behind the desk who, like her surroundings, was in pastel pinks and greys. 'We all want mud baths.'

Another young man came in behind her. For a moment I thought it was the one we had seen earlier in the beauty salon. He seemed to be wearing almost identical clothes. He took Suzan's announcement well, I thought.

'And massage?' he said. 'You all want massage?'

'Why not?' said Suzan.

Harry was still muttering about his penis. Jack said he did not want a massage or a mud bath. He would rather stay in reception and read Plato's *Republic*. When I saw that the cost was $60, I said I thought I might stay in reception and read Plato's *Republic* too. Harry said that no one was going to get him – here he pointed dramatically at the door behind the reception desk – *in there*. Before he could start muttering about his penis again, I said –

'Ned. What about you?'

Ned shrugged.

'Whatever … ', he said.

This is quite often Ned's response to things. If you say to him 'Ned, did you know that the eskimos have three hundred words for snow?' he's quite liable to reply, 'Whatever.' If you ask him to carry in the shopping, or write to his granny, or help with the washing up, there is a strong chance that he will reply, 'Whatever.' I think its roughly equivalent to 'As Allah wills it.' This seemed to be his view of the mud bath. In the end we both agreed to have mud baths, but I said I would take the massage. In a matter of minutes, he and I found ourselves on the other side of the white door, tearing off our clothes and stepping into a large bath of what looked like piping hot cow dung. The man in charge of us was a small Hispanic guy. He had previously been working in the vineyards.

'This is better,' he said. 'Grapes is hard work.'

Like the man who took us out to look at his lorry ticking over in the lorry park, after we tipped out of the bar in Flagstaff, Arizona, he took a touching pride in the way he made his money. When the only bit of either of us visible above the mud line was our heads, he stood, companionably, by the side of the bath, his arms folded, making the sort of determined, blokey conversation that was obviously designed to reassure us that, although we were both stark naked up to our chins in mud, there was nothing funny going on.

The spa room was a long, dark shed, lit rather harshly. The walls were faced with cladding, and the massage rooms on either side of the one corridor were of almost oppressive simplicity. Just behind us on the other side of the room were two large baths of bubbling water.

'World Cup soccer!' said the ex-vineyard worker. 'Good goals, no?'

I nodded. Ned, although he loathes football as much as I do, nodded also.

'My son,' I said, 'is a green belt in karate.' We didn't get much further than this, except that the ex-vineyard worker had worked all over the south-west. He said Flagstaff was a nice place. Phoenix was good too. But he didn't like Calistoga. I asked him why not.

'I got divorced in Calistoga,' he said.

That finished the conversation. Anyway, I was becoming rather over-heated. The mud, which wasn't like mud but more like wet, brown cotton wool, was making my face sweat. Its texture glided over my skin, half-jangle and half-caress, as I pushed my arms and legs deeper into it like a cat stretching into a deep pile carpet.

When we thought we were done the ex-vineyard worker hauled us out and sent us over to the bubbling bath. More naked men arrived and dived into the mud.

'How long do we have to stay here?' Ned said.

'Until they let us out, I suppose,' I said.

Eventually we were allowed to clamber over the side. The ex-vineyard worker led us to two separate cubicles. I lay down and he swathed me in white fluffy towels.

'What do I do now?' I said.

'Just lie there!' said the ex-vineyard worker.

I lay there, waiting for my massage.

I had never been massaged. I had a permanent wave in 1982, but that is about as close as I have ever got to that kind of thing. I didn't really want to have a look at my masseur. I closed my eyes and waited for firm hands to peel back the towels and start slapping my flesh around. Nobody came. Outside I could hear an elderly man discussing his left leg with the ex-vineyard worker. Further along another young man, younger sounding, was discussing money with someone who, as far as I could make out, was doing something to his toes. Still nobody came. They were obviously trying to soften me up. Someone had decided I was a potentially difficult customer and Dr Wilkinson had given the order to leave me swaddled for twenty minutes.

'By the time you get to him,' he told his workers, 'he'll be on his knees begging for massage.'

This was more or less true. As I lay there, wrapped so tightly in the towels that I was not even free to scratch my forehead, I turned over on one side so that I could hear what was going on in the cubicle next to me.

'You're very tense,' a voice was saying; 'you are very tense under my fingers.'

'Whaddever,' said a familiar bass voice.

It was Ned. Clearly someone was massaging, or attempting to massage Ned. And he hadn't even paid for one.

'Are you tense there?' said the voice.

'Possibly,' said Ned.

I didn't like the sound of this. Wriggling violently in order to loosen the towels, I worked myself off the bed and padded out into the corridor. In the next cubicle a plump bearded man was dancing along the side of Ned's bed. Occasionally the man would take out a small phial of bright red liquid and dribble it onto a distinct area of his back. Then, in a slightly effortful manner, he would follow his own index finger and draw it along the lines of Ned's muscles.

'Mr Williams,' said the bearded man, 'I cannot massage you if you're tense!'

'Whaddever,' said Ned into the pillow.

Mr Williams! Of course! The bastard had stolen my $34 massage. My parental feelings were suddenly replaced by a sense of outrage. I had paid good money for what this bearded fraud was doing to Ned, for God's sake! I couldn't, however, somehow summon up the nerve to barge in and demand the next thirteen minutes of digital stimulation. I hovered around in case the bearded man should try anything funny.

'You must lie down!' said the ex-vineyard worker coming towards me. 'You must lie down!'

'I'm fine!' I said.

'You want to go?'

'Yes,' I said, 'I want to go.'

The bearded man was still droning on about how tense Ned was. Was he surprised? Wouldn't he be tense if some guy was dripping red oil onto his spinal cord and doing a soft shoe shuffle immediately due west of his naked back? I went through to the waiting room. I sat on the bench and waited. After a while Ned came through. He looked, I thought, much the same as he had when he went in. Two long brackets of hair fell forwards over his pale cheeks. He sat on the bench next to me.

'You bastard,' I said. 'You stole my massage!'

A slow grin spread across his face.

'Oh, is that what it was?' he said. 'I wondered why that loony was pawing me.'

The grin got bigger. It spread from each corner of his mouth up through his ears, the way it used to do, seventeen years ago, when you were allowed to drop him on the duvet and prod his stomach with your index finger.

'I stole your massage!' he said, as if he had planned the whole thing deliberately.

I found I was grinning too.

'You did, you bastard!' I said. Ned looked me up and down slowly. And he turned and started to put on his clothes.

'Whaddever,' he said. 'Whaddever!'

12

She left her card in San Francisco

As we started to drive down towards San Francisco, Suzan started to make high, squeaking noises. At first I thought they were sounds of alarm, but when I took my eyes off the freeway and fixed them on her, I realized they were a signal of intense pleasure and excitement.

I couldn't work out what was causing them. My driving had improved in the two-and-a-half weeks we had spent in the USA, but I didn't think it was that. 'Look!' she squawked as we started down the broad hill towards the Golden Gate Bridge. 'Look! Look!' I didn't see anything remarkable. There was a wide bay on our left, two huge suspension bridges, one of which seemed to be guiding passengers out into the middle of the waves and leaving them there. Between the two bridges was a densely-packed isthmus of glittering skyscrapers; they picked up the sun and winked back at the white sails of the yachts in the bay, sewn into the blue ocean with the panache of a Dufy.

'Look!' she yelled again. 'Look! Look!'

'Look at what?' I said.

'San Francisco!' she said.

San Francisco, I was to discover, has its publicity well organized: even before she had had the chance to study it, Suzan had enrolled on the city's campaign staff.

'It is amazing!'

She was now shouting quite loudly.

'It is!' Jack was saying. 'It is incredible!'

'Is it?' I said.

I could feel people looking at me.

'Why is it so amazing?' I went on. 'I mean – it's fine. It's a city. But, you know, why is it so incredible?'

A man who can remain unmoved by San Francisco has clearly got something missing. But I am afraid I could not love anyone who could love anyone who could not love San Francisco. I am sorry about this. I'd better get it off my chest before I start telling you about the cable cars and the fog and the San Remo hotel and Pier 31. I am not entirely sure that this confession will ever get beyond the room in which I am writing it. It is possible that my wife and family will sneak into my room at night and burn these shameful sentences before anyone has the chance to see them.

'It didn't seem to do Rudyard Kipling any harm!' Suzan said to me, later, in the Café de Pescatore on North Beach.

'Robert Louis Stevenson loved it!' Jack added.

But I didn't. I didn't like it from the first moment I caught sight of it from the freeway. Or, to be more precise, there was a brief moment when I thought 'This is just another city, isn't it?' And, almost as soon as I let that show in my face, certain others of my party were backing me up against the wall and demanding I swear loyalty to this magical, special place.

I think I would have liked it more if other people had liked it less. It wasn't that I disliked it. It reminded me, for some reason, of Genoa. There may well be a bunch of people who get as excited about Genoa as everyone else seems to get about San Francisco. But they are not as visible.

'This,' said Suzan, as we slowed for the toll, 'is the Golden Gate Bridge.'

'So?' said Ned, who was, I thought, following my lead well.

Suzan gestured wildly.

'It is one of the most famous bridges in the world. It is … ' She thumped the side of the seat.

' … It is huge!'

I thought it was time to ease up on San Francisco. I would lull her into a sense of false security, and then say something moderately pleasant; her only comeback to this would have been to accuse me of not being enthusiastic *enough* – a ploy which would leave me all the room I needed to begin my attempt to demystify what Californians still call The City. I could not, however, resist saying, as we went over –

'It's a bit like the Clifton Suspension Bridge.'

This did not go down well.

We came up the hill that leads towards North Beach. The ocean had disappeared from view. The hill went straight up towards the skyline. The crest of it was a razor's edge of tarmac, as if two slabs of rock had been leant against each other like the floor of a house of cards. We bounced over the top, slammed the bonnet onto the downward slope like a gambler laying out a winning hand, and found we were looking once more at the Pacific. There were grey Victorian houses, as eccentric as suburban castles, garage doors in pastel pink worn pale by salt and wind, and suddenly, in front of us, was a chunky wedge of green metal, packed with people. They looked as if they had hired it for a day's outing. They laughed and joked as if they all knew each other. There was a man in fancy dress at the back, swinging out behind the machine as it ground down the hill on iron rails. With a shock I realized this was not somebody's birthday party or a method of advertising champagne or lingerie, but apparently a respectable form of public transport. Suzan seemed to be having hysterics.

'It's a cable car!' she was yelling. 'It's a cable car!'

She started to sing 'I left my heart in San Francisco'. It wasn't her heart I was worried about her leaving behind. Would she get out of here with her mind intact? Once again we snaked left, then left again. Suddenly we were on a stretch of road as steep as a pass over the Swiss Alps. We went down and down and down and down and down. Then we were in another surprisingly suburban-looking street. Ahead of us was another bus – this time a single-decker with two parallel poles leading up to an overhead wire.

'The Muni,' said Jack, from the rear seat, 'is the nation's first major publicly-owned transportation system. Over 95 per cent of the city's addresses are within two blocks of a moonie. And over 750,000 weekday passengers use Muni. It is America's most heavily-used transportation system on a *per capita* basis!'

'Oh look!' said Suzan. 'There's another one!'

I had never before seen her so excited about the thought of

getting on a bus. You can't usually get her on a bus at all. She's reputed to have got on a number 33A and told it to take her to Flat B, 34 Warrington Grove, Wimbledon. But San Francisco seemed to have changed all that.

We parked the car outside the hotel, just behind Fisherman's Wharf. When I got out I noticed a small but insistent breeze, of the kind that stops you going swimming at English seaside resorts. There seemed to be clouds, too, somewhere up there above the buildings.

'Bit chilly!' I said, in the sort of voice my grandmother used to use if people suggested she moved from her favourite chair. Suzan looked at me with contempt.

'San Francisco is cooler!' she said. She shook out her auburn hair behind her. 'It is the ocean breeze!' she said. I kept a close eye on her as I took out the luggage. She looked as if she was going to start singing again. Maybe even, I thought to myself, dancing.

When I first met her, nearly thirty years ago now, she was walking down The High in Oxford, wearing a mini-skirt and flowers in her hair. I am almost certain there were a few bells in among the flowers. I came to the conclusion that this place had woken some long-dormant hippy gene in her. If I didn't get control quick, she might well be walking down Lombard Street belting out 'Let's go to San Francisco' by the Flower Pot Men, or even more seriously 'If you're going to San Francisco' by Scott McKenzie, from the top of Nob Hill.

To my horror, I found I was singing Scott's UK Number One as I climbed the stairs of the San Remo hotel. Jack was looking at me oddly.

'Did I hear you say,' he said, '"If you're going to San Francisco, you better wear some flowers in your hair, if you're going to San Francisco you're going to meet some gentle people there"?'

'You did,' I said, '"And all across the nation such a strange vibration, umm, people in motion, umm, etc."'

He shook his head.

'You are a sad man!' he said.

'It's all her fault!' I replied, and stomped into my bedroom with our cases.

I lay on the bed and looked out at the street.

There is nothing more telling than the small square of the world you see from a hotel window. From my bedroom at the San Remo Hotel on Mason Street, I could look out at a rectangular section of America that was almost like Europe. There was a man in the apartment opposite. He switched at his net curtains (net curtains!), absorbed in some private reverie, then went away from the glass. He was the first American I'd observed cultivating his privacy. Everything about him and the building he was in – its restraint, its smallness, its muted colours, its fire escape even – was more like Nîmes or Toledo than it was like Needles, Arizona or Boulder City, Nevada. All around me the city smelt of caution and reserve. I no longer felt homesick. I felt glad to be away. Except of course I wasn't away. I was in San Francisco.

San Francisco does more than remind Europeans of home. It demands to be treated like the places they have left. It has a worked-at sense of its cultural identity. Even its skyscrapers demand to be part of the tradition.

'You coming?' said a voice outside.

It was Jack.

'Where to?'

'Shopping, of course!' he said.

I buried my head in the pillow.

'Pier 39!' said Harry, opening the door. 'Apparently there's a shop that just sells left-handed things.'

'I don't want left-handed things!' I said, 'I'm right handed!'

'They may have juggling equipment there!' said Ned.

I struggled to my feet. I went to the small mirror on the wall of my room. Next to it was a neat porcelain wash basin with the kind of antique taps you see in shops on the Fulham Road. ('A family-owned and quiet Italianate Victorian hotel – all rooms share bath facilities reminiscent of Old West inns and European pensions.') I looked at myself. A large red nose. Two small, suspicious blue eyes. A big, white forehead. Cheeks that were a battleground of off-white and pink. The pink seemed to be winning. A forty-six-year-old dad. Go on. Go shopping, dad. What else is there left? Buy juggling equipment, why don't you?

'You coming?' said Suzan's voice.

Women are stronger, I thought, as I went to the door. They shop longer than us.

Out on the street there were people doing something they hardly ever do in Los Angeles – walking. There were bunches of them at the café on the corner. There were crowds of them down by the sea front where the piers jut out into the bay, the seagulls scream wildly at the tourists, and huge, prosperous-looking sea-lions thwacked their tails and fins against floating wooden jetties.

Between us and the sea was a block of public housing. Every other window was boarded up. One window was just open. I stopped by and saw a young black man holding a match to a small circular ball of silver foil. He looked out at me. Behind him I could see a battered wooden table, an unmade bed, and the untended look that goes with poverty. After our eyes had met, he looked back down again at his silver paper, scraped back the foil and started to scratch at the brown resin underneath. With the nutty, over-accented smell of marijuana in my nostrils, I moved on down the street.

Pier 39 is at the north end of the wharfs – a commercial port. It is at the other end of a highway they call the Embarcadero, and is a refurbished wooden pier once used for small fishing boats. As you wander round this uneasy mixture of mall and marina, you realize that it isn't a shopping centre at all. It is a monument to a man called Warren Simpson.

'In the early 1970s, Warren was looking for a waterfront location for his Tia Maria chain of restaurants. He came upon an old pier, Pier 39, which was full of old refrigerators and junk cars.' This elegant fragment of prose is to be found on the place mats of Warren's own restaurant. Did he, I wondered, as I read on, have any hand in its conception? Or was it an entirely spontaneous demonstration of love from Warren's employees?

'Looking past the old refrigerators, Warren envisaged a world-class

waterfront development to brighten the drab San Francisco coast.'

Full of, you know, *boats* and things like that. A place totally lacking in juggling equipment and shops selling leather handbags. Just a lot of dirty men in T-shirts catching fish.

'Our hats off to Warren', went on the place mat, *'for his prescience in bringing such a place into being.'* Or, alternatively, death to Warren for building yet another fucking shopping mall, this time over a decaying wooden structure on the edge of the wild Pacific ocean. What's wrong with old refrigerators and junk cars, Warren? As we wandered round there were other signs that the love his workers felt for Warren just could not be contained. It blossomed into little plaques that told the story of Warren's heroic struggle with political civic groups and red-tape generally. Warren had known, as far back as 1978, that all people really wanted to do was shop.

I went to the side of the pier and looked down at the sea-lions. Occasionally they would lift their whiskered heads up off the wet banks and, stretching their bellies upwards like middle-aged ladies at a fitness class, bark at the windy sea around them. Sometimes one of them would take exception to another and try to shove him (or her) off the wood and into the sea. It was hard to tell why they did this. As far as I could make out, sometimes the one who had been shoved off would slither back up from the other end without showing signs of resentment. The basic thing was to do your air force exercises and make a noise like a rusty winch. I was looking down at the sea-lions, and feeling good about the fact that I had my back to Warren's monument to his own persistence, when I heard feet thudding behind me along the wooden boards. I turned to see Suzan, closely followed by Ned, Jack and Harry. She had her head well down, and was making jerky movements with her left arm; her right shoulder was lifted at an angle as if she were carrying a rifle or a spade, like one of Snow White's seven dwarfs. The boys, too, had a determined military air. It was clear that something pretty serious had happened out there in Warren's world-class waterfront development. She stopped when she got within a few yards of me and said –

'They took it away!'

She didn't say what they had taken away, but Ned said –

'Her Visa card. They took it away.'

He looked menacing.

'Bastards. I'd like to smash them.'

Jack and Harry said they, too, would like to smash them. Harry was doing quite a lot of sideways slicing of the air with his right hand.

'Let me deal with this,' I said in frank, manly tones. 'He took away your card? He has no right to do that.'

There was a lot of muttering from the lads. A sea-lion pushed another sea-lion into the water.

'He has absolutely no right to do that.'

I was beginning to get worked up. The louder my voice got, I noticed, the calmer they became.

'He has absolutely no bloody *right*!'

'Calm down!' said Suzan.

'I will not calm down!' I said. 'I am angry. I am very, very, very angry.'

She cheered up at this news.

'Where is this man?' I said.

'Oh, he's quite *nice*,' Suzan said. 'He was very nice about it … '

'Nice?' I snarled. 'Nice? He's *nice*? I don't think so. I don't *think* so … '

I, too, started to do small but aggressive things with my hands.

'Take me to him,' I said. 'I will talk to him. I'll do more than talk to him. I will tell him he has absolutely no *right*!'

Jack started to say something about the rules governing the use and abuse of credit cards. No one paid any attention to him. The five of us, shoulder to shoulder, marched off through the crowds of shoppers. The breeze was still coming in from the sea. To the south beyond the Bay Bridge, a cigar-shaped line of fog hung in curious isolation over the ocean. When we got to the shop, I pushed open the doors. There were two men and a girl behind the counter. A young black man, a middle-aged man with a moustache and a girl of about twenty.

'Which one is it?'

'Him!' Suzan hissed, pointing at the man with the moustache. 'He's quite nice, actually … '

Before I had time to compose my expression, the man with the moustache was coming towards me.

'I've come,' I said sternly, 'for my wife's credit card.'

'Yes?' he said.

'I want it back!' I went on.

'Yes!' he said.

I folded my arms.

'There's been a mistake,' I said, 'and we demand this card be returned!'

'Sure!' he said.

This was proving easier than I had anticipated. I held up my open palm. Into it he placed Suzan's Visa card. It was in four pieces. I looked at it.

'You've cut it up!' I said.

I sounded, I thought, not as strong as I would like to have sounded.

'Yes,' he said.

'Why?' I said.

I started to say something about our account being in credit, and how we came from London, England and all he had to do was telephone the National Westminster Bank, Leatherhead, Surrey. 'They know me there!' I said. 'I am a personal friend of the manager.'

He didn't seem very impressed by this. He spoke as to a small child.

'You see,' he said, 'we ring a number. We ring a toll-free number. And they tell us we have to cut up the card.'

I sniffed.

'They,' I said. 'Who are "they" exactly? What exactly do "they" … '

He spoke again – very slowly and clearly.

'I don't know who they are exactly,' he said. 'It's just a number we ring. They are in Nebraska. And if they tell us to do it, we have to do it.'

Were they perhaps members of an alien civilization? An outreach department of the Mafia? I started to try and tell him, once again, about my very solid relationship with the manager of the National Westminster Bank, Leatherhead. He still did not seem interested.

'Look,' I said, 'give me their number. I will ring them. I don't think they have any right to order you to cut up cards like that.'

'We have to do it,' he went on, rather cravenly. 'We ring them and if they tell us to cut up your card, then we have to obey them.'

'And if they tell you to take off your trousers and run round the Embarcadero shouting "I am a chicken", you do that, do you? Who the hell do they think they are?' He gave a toll-free number and, clutching the pieces of Suzan's Visa card, I stormed out of the shop and ran to the nearest phone box.

The people in Nebraska were as vague as the shop manager about who they were.

'I can't comment on that,' said the woman who answered the phone as I started to try and speak to her. 'All I can say is that the card has been declined.'

'It has more than been declined,' I screamed, 'it's been cut into tiny little pieces by a man with a moustache!'

I started to try and tell her about the manager of the National Westminster Bank, Leatherhead. She seemed about as indifferent to him as the man with the moustache had been. I was beginning to feel uncomfortably English. I was 4,000 miles away from Leatherhead. They had started to move in on Suzan's credit card. Maybe mine would be next. Maybe they would come for me back at the San Remo Hotel.

'Look,' said the woman in Nebraska, 'all I can say is there has been an instruction from someone in regard to your card.'

'From Leatherhead!' I said.

She wouldn't say. She presumably spent her days up there in Nebraska, fielding calls just like this from all over the world. Maybe Suzan, unknown to me, had gone on a binge-buy of garden equipment at Mark Torlock's Garden Centre, Wimbledon. Maybe she was leading a double life with this Visa card. Maybe …

We went back to the hotel. I said I was going to ring up the bank manager and shout at him. Suzan said it was three in the morning in Leatherhead. I said I would ring Visa and shout at them. Suzan said it was three in the morning in Southend as well. I said I would ring somebody and shout at them. She said she didn't mind who I shouted at so long as it wasn't her. She said it was her card, not mine. I wondered whether she had been doing things with it. She said what things. I accused her of taking men out to lunch. Then I accused her of buying garden equipment. Then she told me that I was as bad as the man who had cut up the card. She said credit was always in the hands of men. Somewhere at the bottom of all this, she said darkly, was a middle-aged man. In the end we gave up and went out to eat.

Much, much later we discovered it was all a mistake. But I am afraid San Francisco will always be, for me, the place where my wife's Visa card was destroyed. We did go in a cable car. We went down to Union Square, spent a morning at the Exploratorium, watched a moonie driver try to hitch up his trolley bus to the overhead wire, went out to Alcatraz Island where we shuffled round the cells and sat looking back towards the city as Al Capone must have done, marvelling at its closeness.

We went down Haight Street and saw kids sitting out on the sidewalk, sitting by dustbins, no flowers in their hair. Later on, I was chased by two black youths – the only ones I have ever met who addressed me as 'White Boy'. We climbed Nob Hill and the boys commented, at some length, on its name. We went to Chinatown and Japantown (which reminded me, for some reason, of Hendon) and eventually we drove out on the road south, towards Highway 101, Big Sur, Monterey and Santa Cruz. But for me, San Francisco will always be the place where my wife left her credit card.

13

Roads and plains and the big city at night

One of the things I didn't like about The City was its weather. I was never sure what to wear. If you go out in a jersey in San Francisco you end up having to tie it around your waist, or attach it to some part of your body that might well be a secret signal to San Francisco's flourishing gay community (one of the lads – he is asking me not to name him – said on day two at the San Remo hotel that he 'wanted to go and look at them'. When we said 'who?', he said 'the gays'. I think he thought they were a tourist attraction like the fog or the cable cars).

I wanted California to be sun and sand and surf. I wanted, I said to Suzan as we drove south down Highway 101, to drive my custom machine to the drive-in. I wanted to be with the Beach Boys, I said, checking my board on to my woody and catching a big one off Malibu. Suzan was quite negative about the Beach Boys. She said they were for old people.

But the country south of San Francisco encourages a man to dream about suntanned bodies and beautiful coastlines, perhaps because it is, for the most part, made up of precisely those things. We went down 101 and then turned west towards Santa Cruz; as soon as we came into that town, between the hills and the blue ocean, I knew I was where I wanted to be. There was a single-engine plane towing someone on a paraglider. There was a pier. There was sand. There was an ocean whose waves curled lazily into the beach, like the beaches at Bournemouth when I was a child. There was a feeling of safety and permanence. Jack looked up from the guide. Since finishing Plato's *Republic* (which he announced was 'quite good', except that Plato was 'probably insane'), he had been studying books on America.

'Santa Cruz,' he said, 'is where old hippies come to die.'

'That's me!' I said.

We swam, lay on the beach and headed south to Monterey.

'In Monterey,' said Suzan brightly as we pulled away, 'there is an aquarium.'

Harry said he did not want to look at fish. Suzan told him he liked fish. 'You all like fish. Ned used to love fish!' she said. 'Do you remember that aquarium in Wales? You were only five. You loved it.' Harry said once again that he did not like fish. They made him nervous, he said. Ned and Jack, perhaps wisely, stayed out of this debate.

I was very much on Suzan's side. I have always liked fish. I like watching them. I like eating them. And I like looking at them in large, spotlit glass cases. Whatever form my relation with them takes, it is never an intense one. One might as well, one feels, be eating them as looking at them. And vice versa. I like the way they ignore you. I like the way they swim past, gulping at invisible food, as you press your nose to the glass.

'There'll be squid!' I said, with slightly forced jollity. 'And octopus! And sharks!'

Before the war Monterey Bay played host to very large numbers of sardines. They swam around the bay and, as far as I can gather, the guys just scooped them up and shoved them into tins. John Steinbeck, who was born at Salinas not far from Monterey, wrote about the workers who came to the coast to deal with these creatures. Then, after the war, the sardines mysteriously disappeared. The book seemed to suggest that they had all, as one man, woken up one morning and decided Monterey was not for them. Jack said he thought it more likely that they had fished them so hard they had wiped them out. In the 1950s I can remember an awful lot of sardines. They were a not-always-welcome feature of an enormous number of meals. You got them on toast. They cropped up in salads at school, lying in wait for you behind damp lettuce leaves. Sometimes they were coated in a kind of red slime. Sometimes (I seem to remember) they came out of their tin with the heads still in place – their expressionless eyes and crumbling backbones haunting your mealtime until you thought that, like the royal family, sardines would always be there.

Well – now they are in a large tank in the Monterey aquarium and schoolchildren sit in front of them writing projects about them. Cannery Row, a street that gave Steinbeck the name of one of his most famous novels, is now made up of restaurants and craft shops. After we were through with the aquarium and watched a curator swim out in an open-air tank and pick shells off the bottom, we went out to the waterfront. There were a few wreaths of fog out on the open sea. On the harbour was a blackened lean-to, in front of which was a sign advertising whale watching. There was one fishing boat out on the pier next to Fisherman's Wharf. Two guys in jeans and T-shirts were sorting out fish as if they were clothes for a jumble sale. There were piles of silver ones, piles of bright red ones and, on the corner, an octopus.

'They'll beat it out on the rocks now!' I said.

Suzan shuddered.

They did no such thing. They started to throw the smaller fish into the water. From behind a nearby boat, a small flock of pelicans emerged. They had thick, dirty white feathers. Their beaks were the size of an orang-utan's stomach. Their eyes were watchful in an almost human way. As the two fishermen threw fish, they swooped down and snapped them up. This seemed to amuse the two men. A small crowd gathered. The two seemed to enjoy playing to an audience. On one end of the boat, like a crumpled plastic coat covered in slime, was a jellyfish. One of them levered it up with the end of a boat hook and tipped it over the side. The two men laughed. The crowd gathered on the quay laughed too. For a moment I thought I was looking at a Mediterranean scene – the kind of thing you might see on one of the Greek islands. And then something about the two men – their fashionable jeans, perhaps, the jaunty modernity of their T-shirts, or just the way in which they treated their audience as equals, sharing in their routine – reminded me that in America there are no peasants, there are only potential millionaires. Their fishing smack, no more than thirty or forty feet long, its tiny wheelhouse painted a drab white, its broad bows chaffing restlessly on the pier, waiting for the next trial of strength with the ocean beyond the bay, wasn't – as it might have been in Naxos or Falmouth – the end of something. It was a beginning.

If Americans have stopped selling things to the world, it is not because they are not capable of it. They are simply bored with it. They made motor cars. More cars than anywhere else in the world were turned out by towns in Michigan that are now as dead as Calico, where, when they had pulled all the silver out of the desert, they went on and tried something else. They did silver. Why do silver? They did cars. Why do cars? The Japanese do cars now. Does that make them special? And the Americans, who invented all this stuff – who thought of hairdryers and dishwashers and refrigerators, stereos and stretch limousines – have, like many other ingenious nations, been left high and dry by their own cunning. They sit among the driftwood dreaming of something new.

It's such an exhausting, romantic country for a European. All European cultures (which, of course, include Japan) are based on the idea of accepting one's limitations. The feudal relationship ties us to countries that are superficially even more distant from us than the Japanese – India, China, almost the whole of the globe east of Turkey. Feudalism is the romantic re-working of a theory of society based on obligation. That element of obligation, of accepting the limitations of duty, and deciding that loyalty to a state can be exactly the same as loyalty to a friend or relative, is fundamental to almost any state you could care to name until the late eighteenth century. And all revolutions – whether in France, England, Russia or anywhere else – have been followed by a nervous return to an enhanced version of precisely those values they had seemed designed to overthrow.

It is only in America, where Jeffersonian democracy was and is the basis of the state, that a durable, exportable version of revolution has been created. American ideas about equality and obligation are, as Tiananmen Square demonstrated, the most subversive on the planet. The notion that free men, equal before the law, are *the basis of the constitution itself*, seems to be the most revolutionary one we have come up with yet. I thought about this as we walked towards the car.

'Are there any poor people in America?' said Harry, picking up my mood. 'Or are they all rich?'

I reminded him of the woman we had seen in a back street of San Francisco. She was picking up tin cans, pounding them flat and then putting them in a plastic bag. I reminded him of the housing we had seen in downtown LA as we lost our way off Airport Boulevard.

'I suppose,' said Harry, 'they keep the poor people separate from the rich people. And we're the rich people.'

It was hard to argue with this. Harry has the moral clarity I have noticed in people of his age. I didn't want to get into a long argument about welfare schemes or taxation or unemployment levels. I certainly didn't want to get into discussing President Clinton – who over here seemed even more improbable than he had looked in London. So we did what all good Americans do when faced by a problem. We climbed into our red Ford Aerostar. We buckled up and we headed on south towards Santa Barbara. We drove, with the ocean on our right, down to a place called Cambria. We took a trip to Hearst Castle. Here the American newspaper magnate William Randolph Hearst constructed an enduring monument to bad taste, in which mediaeval rood screens, obscure seventeenth-century portraits and looted or duplicated Roman statuary sit uneasily next to fake Moorish courtyards and the kind of armchairs found in English private hotels.

'Mr Hearst,' said our guide, showing us a dining-room table that looked as if it had been made out of off-cuts from a Venetian galley, 'always made a point of having ketchup on the table.'

He was also, as far as I could make out, the kind of guy who would hang a Piero della Francesca on his lavatory wall – just to show he could do it. The guide, as is so often the case, was far more interesting than the place she was showing us. She was also, I decided, got up in much better taste. What was charming about her was the pride and enthusiasm she was prepared to demonstrate on behalf of a place that proved absolutely nothing apart from the fact that, if you have a lot of money, you can buy a lot of things. As far as she was concerned Mr Hearst – as she insisted on calling him – was what she or we or anyone could become if they got off their arses and made sure they had a daddy who owned a very large chunk of the central coast of California.

We sat in a restaurant outside Cambria and looked at the sunset. The ocean made the huge, red disc seem unnervingly close as it settled into the waves of the Pacific. We drove on south, still with the ocean on our right, past Big Sur, where wild country faces a wilder sea. We stayed a night in Santa Barbara where, in the room next to ours, I saw a beautiful girl drop her luggage onto the floor and burst into tears.

'If I had known we were going to Santa Barbara,' she said to the tall, handsome man who was waiting for her in the room, 'I never would have come.'

But I didn't see any real poverty or pain or distress on the road; I had found the California I dreamed about when Michael Wear, Michael Wood and I played *Pet Sounds* on our record-players, and played it over and over again on a hot summer afternoon in the late 1960s. When we drove past something called the San Luis Obispo Mens' Colony, I told the family it was probably a therapy centre where huge bearded men would hug each other and learn how to express themselves by touching and feeling. It turned out to be a prison. I stood on the beach at Malibu, watching a small blonde kid, clutching his board, thrust himself into the surf; watching a beautiful girl ride a wave as long as a cricket pitch and slide gracefully into the shallows, while behind her beach boys like elegant flotsam paddled in the huge breakers. The coast from Carmel to the John Paul Getty museum, where Highway 101 meets the western end of Sunset Boulevard, passed by in a kind of dream.

Los Angeles seemed almost like home.

We were staying in the Mondrian Hotel on Sunset Boulevard, just across the street from the Chateau Marmont. In the lobby the concierge, a tanned young man of about twenty-eight, was telling a guest about the car he had hired for him. He seemed as enthusiastic about its road-holding, its upholstery and its luxury fittings as if he was going to drive it himself. From high up in the hotel, we looked out over the city. We were due to fly out that night.

'It hasn't changed,' said Suzan as we watched the sky grow dim behind the distant buildings.

'No,' I said, 'I don't think it has.'

I lay on the bed and thought about all this. I thought about America. I thought about voice mail and ice dispensers and a chat show I had seen on television where an audience shouted at a mother who they thought was bringing her daughter up wrong. They seemed especially worried about the fact that the mother was a stripper and ran a sex shop. I thought about how, a mere three weeks ago, I had been puzzled at the sight of the word PEDXING laid out on the road in front of me in the direction of travel (in England it would have been laid out in precisely the opposite way). I thought about how American telephones not only spoke to you but asked you complicated questions, and quite often told you which of their buttons to press. I thought about how, in San Francisco, I had tried to book cinema tickets over the phone and spent twenty minutes choosing options which, in the end, returned me politely and courteously to the point where I had started.

Down below by the swimming pool, a tiny square of blue from nineteen floors up, there was a highschool reunion going on. A lot of young, successful, well-dressed Americans were being politely pleased to see each other again. I thought about hash browns and regular coffee and roll-away beds and the radio station in Arizona where a man spent the whole day talking about the love of Jesus.

Then I put on my hat.

It was the hat from the store in Chinle, Arizona – the one that was an exact replica of the hat I had glimpsed on at least three different Indian heads in Window Rock. I have only worn it once since returning to England – in Richmond Park, after dark. It's a hat designed to be worn by men who herd cattle or ride young bulls, clutching their horns as they buck crazily around the rodeo. But in America I wore it almost all the time.

Sometimes I had worn it in bed. In Boulder City, Nevada, I had kept it on even while I was in the closet section of the mens' lavatory. I pulled it down over my eyes and went to look at myself in the mirror.

'I'm an Amurkan!' I said.

'No you're not!' said Suzan.

'I'm from the Wild West,' I said.

Suzan looked up at me. She didn't seem at all impressed by the hat, even if it had cost nearly $180.

'You can't wear that hat on the east coast,' she said. 'They'll laugh at you.'

I said I didn't care. I went to the window and looked back out over Los Angeles. I thought, but didn't say, that I was beginning to understand this country. But, as I was to discover, it's only when you start to think you've got the hang of the place, that it really begins to surprise you.

14

The great New England tree conspiracy

I had never expected there to be quite so many trees in New England.

I had read about them, of course. I had seen pictures of them. I had even heard that, in what we call Autumn and they call the Fall, New England was the place to go. But the full extent of the tree problem did not really become clear to me until I drove from Kennedy Airport to Cape Cod, and from Cape Cod up to Vermont, and from Vermont down into Connecticut, and from Connecticut down into New York State. I didn't get into Maine, but from what I hear of that, the tree epidemic is, if anything, even more serious than in the other states of New England.

We flew out of LAX in the early evening and arrived in New York at midnight local time. Perhaps that was why I found the trees so surprising. I didn't feel we had travelled at all. Even the electric storm, as we came into the airport, didn't seem real. I half expected, as we got out of the plane, to see more of the desert hills of the West Coast. Instead there were queues of anxious-looking people waiting for buses and taxis and, in the forecourt, the remains of what looked like a tropical storm. As I stepped over the puddles I heard voices from wisecracking comedies – the nasal, aggressive tones of people who enjoy arguments for their own sake. 'Whaddya mean there's *no bus*!' a man over to my left was saying.

We had decided to end our trip by staying in New York. We had planned to drive out north-west of Kennedy without touching the city. And, after the scrum at the terminal building, the queue in the Hertz office seemed almost English in its gentility. Perhaps, I thought, as we waited in line, this is New England *politesse*. I couldn't work out what it was, but something –

frankness perhaps, a certain kind of spontaneity – had evaporated in the five-hour flight into the darkness and against the clock. Behind me was a man who sold real estate.

'The Japanese,' he told me, 'are worth more in property terms than the whole of the United States.' I tried to look impressed by this.

'What about the Grand Canyon?' he said. 'Can you put a value on the Grand Canyon?' This seemed, I thought, a slightly defeatist attitude for an estate agent. Indeed, I met more than a few Americans who failed to qualify as ambassadors for capitalism. They seemed to me to be much more like the conventional view of an imperial nation that has lost its way – like the English: resigned, wry, concerned with higher things.

The trees started not long after we drove out from Kennedy along the Van Wyck expressway, and across the Triborough bridge that takes you back over the Hudson river and towards New England.

As I piloted the Lincoln Continental nervously through a maze of green signs, distant lights and darkened lanes that merged in front of and behind me, I asked the rest of the party if they could see New York.

'No!' yelled Suzan. 'It's dark! It's dark! Keep your eyes on the road!'

Occasionally a pair of headlights would come at me from the blackness. Sometimes they would come up on the right or the left and slip past me and on into the gloom. Sometimes they seemed to be coming straight at me. Sometimes the driver, or the passengers, looked back, amused at the big white car driving as nervously as an old lady towards Connecticut.

At the Triborough Bridge, bathed in lurid neon, my first New Yorker (if you didn't count the man at the Hertz desk) waited for her toll. I said I thought she looked less friendly than people in the West. Suzan said that if I were taking tolls at two in the morning, I would probably not bother to establish much of a relationship with my customers.

Then we were over the river. There were no more lights. But the trees began.

My first view of them was in the headlights of the car. But, even before the lamps picked them out, you could sense them, muffling the highway. Sometimes you were aware that, over to your left, was a black shape. Sometimes a lighter patch of sky at the edge of the road would pick out a line of objects that were obviously trees, and then, later, when you were looking straight into the eye of the night, you could tell that, to right and left of you, massed like an army waiting for orders, there were yet more of the damn things. You didn't worry about this at first. You knew there were supposed to be trees in New England. You were not even particularly surprised when, after turning off the freeway towards a small town called Darien, there were even more of them.

Close up, they looked like the kind of trees you might find at home. I don't know what they were – birch, or beech maybe. I have never been very knowledgeable about trees. But by now it was obviously irrelevant what species they were. Their individuality had been completely absorbed in the colossal scale of their presence. There was something almost offensive about the way they lounged around in front of the square-cut houses (painted, for the most part, yellow or green, perhaps in an attempt at camouflage), as if pretending to be ordinary normal *trees* instead of part of a massive conspiracy.

Because (at three in the morning) a conspiracy is what they almost certainly were. The trees were the ones in charge round here. There was no horizon. There was no way of telling whether you were going up or down or north or south or east or west. There was only a mysterious, green corridor. And when you did finally reach a settlement of some kind, it seemed to have been laid out in deference to the trees. There was no village green, no pub, no break in the forest, just a brief, hesitant line of shops that reminded me of the kind of thing you might see in Surrey or Hampshire – and then another few billion trees.

We came upon Darien (where we were due to spend what was left of the night) almost by accident. We found we had driven through it before it had even begun. There was no sign of the Comfort Inn, the motel chain where I had reserved one room with five beds. But because the town itself was such a tentative presence, fading as deftly as Robin Hood's Merry Men into the forest at the first sign of a stranger, we kept expecting it to start up again. Certainly one or two of the houses, with the illuminated windows of children's clothes shops, seemed, after we had passed them, to move swiftly and silently through the dark trees to our right and reposition themselves on the road ahead. Unlike in Arizona, where a bare noticeboard thrust into the desert would tell you in plain words NEEDLES CITY LIMITS, Darien, Connecticut was not keen to let you know where you stood.

We had driven on for about ten minutes, and were passing a few more wooden houses which hid, like the witch's place in Hansel and Gretel, in the all-embracing forest, when Suzan said –

'I don't think we're in Darien any more. We'd better turn round.'

We turned round and drove back down the road. It was the road I thought we had just travelled along, but Darien seemed to have melted back into the greenery. The trees, I decided, were in on this. It was they that had moved, not the buildings. At any moment they would creep up and stand round us in a deadly crescent, like the wood in Auden's poem. After a while we came back to Highway 95. The trees here had arranged themselves with beguiling sparseness, and with relief at the thought that I had finally shaken them off, I pushed the Lincoln back onto the carriageway. All we had to do was drive back down the highway until we saw a sign to Darien.

'We won't see a sign to Darien,' said Suzan; 'we've just been through it.'

'We've either been through it backwards or forwards,' I said. 'If we've been through it backwards, we'll see a sign for Darien. If we've been through it forwards, we'll see a sign for the next town after Darien, which is … '

'I don't know. Boston,' said Suzan, 'or New York. Depending on which way we're going, I suppose.'

I would have asked her if there were any distinguishing features about the landscape on either side of the freeway, but there seemed little point. The trees had taken care of that department.

154

We drove on in a direction that could have been north-west or south-east, but there were no signs to Darien or to Norwalk or Stamford, the towns that would tell us in which direction we were headed. Instead, after about four miles of trees, we were offered a town that neither of us could find anywhere in either the Michelin Guide to New England, the Fodor's Guide to the South West Coast of Connecticut, or Hansford's easily-accessible map of the East Coast of the USA.

'Go to it anyway!' yelled Suzan. 'Then at least we'll know which way we're facing!'

'How will we know,' I yelled back, 'until we know where we are?' By now we had passed the turn-off for wherever it was to which we would have been heading if we had taken it. We were still yelling at each other when Jack said – 'Look! Darien!'

And then, like people in a dream, we found ourselves going back down the same turn-off we had taken earlier, driving through the same eerily-neat row of shops and houses, and watching the town be taken over once more by the ubiquitous trees without having given us a clue as to where we were. Or where the Comfort Inn might be. Were we going to repeat this manoeuvre over and over again throughout the night, until the trees finally closed in round us? How would we ever escape the cursed circle in which we seemed trapped? It was then that Jack pointed out that there was a phone in the car. I dialled the number of the Comfort Inn, Darien.

'Where am I?' I said, after the preliminary courtesies.

It was now a quarter-past-three in the morning.

'I don't know,' said a sleepy voice, 'you tell me. Is there a fire station near you? Have you passed a fire station?'

'I'm not sure,' I said.

The woman at the end of the line seemed as vague about Darien as I was.

'There are trees everywhere!' I said. 'All over the place. Hundreds of trees!'

She went to fetch someone else. A man with a hoarse voice came on the line. He, too, seemed keen on the fire station. But, by now, we were back in the heart of the trees. I can't remember how he talked us down to the Comfort Inn. All I do remember is, when we finally got there, it turned out to be just off an approach road from the main freeway. We had passed it three or four times before in the course of the night's drive.

'We must have passed it on our way into town,' said Suzan. 'If it hadn't been for the trees, we'd have seen it.'

The trees were there the next morning. They looked, I thought, even more smug by day than they had done the night before. They crowded up to our window. They had relented enough to allow the Comfort Inn to build a tarmac car-park and, when we turned out onto it next morning, at first they kept a discreet distance. But by the time we got back to Highway 95, they were up to their old tricks.

I had thought that, by daylight, they might seem livelier. I wasn't expecting them to start doing a Mexican wave or thrashing about in the breeze, or suddenly turning yellow and brown in order to give us a sneak preview of what they might look like come the Fall (further on up the road I saw a sign giving a radio frequency to tune to if you wanted to hear something called Foliage Reports), but I had not expected them just to stand there, sullenly, on either side of 95, dumbly following the slow lines of hills and valleys. I hadn't expected them either to be quite such a uniform shade of green. And I had expected them to be a bit more forthcoming about their identity.

'What are they?' I said to Suzan. 'Birch or beech, or what?'

'I don't know,' she answered. 'Watch the road.'

New England was making everyone very bad tempered. And, by the time we got to Mystic Seaport ('A lot to see, much to do, welcome aboard!'), there was a strong feeling that trees weren't the only thing wrong with Connecticut.

'It's a bit like England,' said Harry, as we drove past the shabby edges of New Haven. 'It sort of just goes on and on, and then there's some buildings. And the people aren't so friendly.'

Mystic, Connecticut, is the other side of New Hampshire. In the nineteenth century it was home to ships and boatyards – some of the tallships were in the large open-air museum on the banks of the Mystic river.

In California, I had the impression that anything might happen at any moment. In New England I had exactly the contrary feeling. It seemed as if everything had already occurred, and it was the duty of the population to remind us of that fact. The selling of the past has become a mania with the British, but there is something particularly disturbing for an Englishman about the form re-packaged history takes on the East Coast.

At first I thought it might be thwarted colonial pride. We'd been driving through a territory that evoked the War of Independence. Norwalk, for example, is the home of the Yankee Doodle Dandies, and we were on our way to the city that gave the British the Boston Tea Party. And yet I had the obstinate feeling that it was New England, not me, that had failed to understand its own past. That its take on the US Constitution was still too English to make sense of the gob-smackingly simple idea of the heart of America. The writers of the Eastern elite – the ones who rule the pages of the *New York Review of Books* – do exude a cultural confidence that isn't really cultural confidence at all. When John Updike asked his famous question about Kingsley Amis's *Lucky Jim* ('What is it for?'), he wasn't simply displaying his lack of a sense of humour (always, as far as I could see, a safe thing to do in New England), he was simply representing the Puritan assumptions of the place. Everything must have its use – even adultery, in Updike's case anyway. Everything has to look as if it's for the good of the community. Right-thinking men and women having good and useful thoughts. That was the smell in the air at Mystic anyway, and I didn't like it.

I went to the boathouse at the edge of the river and was greeted by three or four people of the kind you see officiating at village fêtes in England. The labour-intensive nature of this transaction reminded me, too, of eastern Europe before the collapse of communism. There was a little bearded guy and a big woman in a brown suit and an elderly lady in a jumper and skirt and a young girl.

'I'd like,' I said, 'to hire a rowing boat.'

They nodded slowly. The elderly lady and the young girl looked at the little bearded guy. 'I DON'T NORMALLY DO THIS,' his every gesture screamed, 'I HAVE ANOTHER LIFE.' As he came towards me I noticed that he was wearing a small badge that told me who he was. He waited for me to finish trying to read it and then he engaged my eyes. I got the impression he was going to ask me something very, very serious.

'Do you have skills?' he said.

I wasn't sure what he meant by this.

'I have rowed,' I said. 'I rowed up the Thames. From London to Oxford.'

He nodded slowly.

'I wrote a book about it!' I said. 'It was published. In England.'

He nodded again.

'You are an oarsman, then,' he said in level tones.

He handed me a sheet of paper. It set out, at some length, the qualifications required for taking out a rowing boat on the Mystic river. There were quite a few of them. They didn't hire these boats out to just anybody. As well as having perfect eyesight, a clean driving licence, a degree from Harvard and a Master Mariner's diploma, you had to promise not to smoke or behave lewdly and not to insult the American flag while piloting your craft. Or that's what it felt like. When I had signed the document in triplicate, the bearded guy nodded to one of his assistants.

'As captain of this vessel,' he said, 'you need to know a few things about the Mystic river.' It is chock-full of sharks. It flows backwards. Whatever it was he had to say, it was clearly pretty serious. We went to the front of his little shack and looked out at it. It did look delightful. It's a small river. It reminded me for some reason of the Helford river in Cornwall. I didn't mind this, but once again I felt a slight disappointment. I hadn't come all this way just to look at a large-scale version of English provincial.

'You must,' said the bearded man, 'keep to the left of the green buoys.' That left me a narrow channel over by the right bank. It led past the jetty to an iron bridge, beyond which was a path and the sea. The miniature estuary, only a few hundred yards across at its widest point, was studded with boats and fringed with green trees. The water had done something to the trees. Down here towards the beginning of the grey-blue horizon, the astonishing prairie of sea and sky, they were almost bearable.

'You may not go beyond the bridge,' he said, 'and you may not go up beyond where we are now standing.'

It would probably have been simpler to tie the thing up, sit in it for a couple of minutes and hand the man $15.

'And,' he said, 'you must all wear a lifejacket.'

He and the lady in the brown suit went out to the jetty where the young girl was hauling in the rowing boat. The five of us stood on the dock while he read us the marine equivalent of our Miranda rights. When we tried to climb aboard he told us we had to get on in reverse order. Since we didn't know what he thought the order should be, it took another five minutes for him to explain. By the time we got on to the boat we were too demoralized to do anything apart from creep in a decorous half-circle across the bay while our bearded friend watched us through binoculars from the boathouse. The whole occasion was, once again, unnervingly English. Suzan said later she thought the whole place – and she meant New England, not just Mystic Connecticut – seemed to be run by the sort of woman who does well in the run-up to the King's College Wimbledon Christmas Craft Fayre.

I had in my head a picture of the New England of Melville and Robert Lowell. But it wasn't until we got much further west that I saw the Atlantic in all its glory. And it was only then that I understood how someone could think New England beautiful. The trees were there, OK, but as we came down towards Cape Cod, a crooked finger of land stretching out into the Atlantic from the far west point of Massachusetts, they started to yield to the horizon. As soon as we drove along the cape the road rose above them, a safe passage through the massed ranks of green, and we became more and more aware of the enormous grey space to our right.

Years ago I was staying in the west of Ireland, camped on a cliff near a village in Connemara. One day an old boy from the village came up and looked out at the sea, and as he watched the limitless water and sky, he whispered, almost to himself, 'Yes. The wide Atlantic.' Over here there seemed to be almost more sea, because there was more shore.

We turned off the through road down towards Hyannis Port. From Hyannis we drove along the southern side of the cape looking out towards Nantucket. A few miles east of Hyannis is Chatham. Although by now the shops that looked like barns, the locals who looked like tourists and the countryside that looked like someone's back garden were starting to annoy me, at Chatham there was, unequivocally, the sea. At Chatham Bars – a long spit of sand stretching out into the bay protecting it from the Atlantic beyond – we stayed for three days in a room facing the ocean. We didn't go back into the town at all. We sat on the beach all day – once we sailed out to the sand bars and walked with the officious gulls through the shallows that, at high tide, would swallow this last stretch of land between us and Connemara. In the evening we sat in a restaurant, still facing out to the sea, eating clams and tuna and lobster, watching the lights of boats come and go as the sky went purple-grey to thick black. The Pacific ocean is for leisure. Even the big ships moored at San Francisco looked as if they were out for a good time. But the Atlantic is for work. At last that Puritan spirit started to seem interesting. Picket fences and all the snobbery of Boston were at our backs – we only had eyes for the limitless expanse of grey water and rain, calm, storm, sunshine, coming in across towards us from the only place in New England where no trees grow.

15

It is a gift to be complex, it is a gift to be devious

I had the idea that, if I got to Vermont, the landscape would change.

I don't know why this should have been the case. I hadn't seen pictures of how things were up there. I suppose I could have got hold of some. But that would have spoiled things. I had heard someone say 'Up in Vermont', and for reasons I didn't quite understand, I had decided that it was a place where there would be primitive farms, sturdy, decent, plain folks, and muddy lanes like the roads in rural Hertfordshire in my childhood. I had decided it would be a place like England was before National Car Parks got hold of it and squeezed it until it choked.

God knows why I thought this. It must have been some form of travel fatigue. I had absolutely no basis for thinking any of these things. It was simply to do with the sound of the word Vermont.

And once again, on the basis of the word, we took a long journey. We drove in a single day all the way from Cape Cod up through Boston (which I saw from the freeway) towards Vermont. It was freeway most of the way, but further north in Massachusetts we got onto something called the Housatonic trail, which claimed to be something to do with Indians. It was a two-lane black-top, rather like an English country road. I saw no Indians, apart from a large model of one stuck by the side of the road to let you know they were a factor here as well. Somebody I met later in a bar in a place called North Adams, up closer to Vermont, told me that the East Coast Indians were doing very well. 'They're allowed to open casinos,' he said in slightly envious tones. 'They are coining it. They all have names like Snipes and MacArthur, but if they can prove they're

Indians they can coin it. They're allowed gambling licences.'

It is certainly true that there have been several cases in which ancient treaty rights were fought through the courts. But you have to have enough money to find the right kind of lawyer. *Indian America*, by the Choctaw Irish artist and writer called Eagle/Walking Turtle or Gary McClean, depending upon who's talking to him, lists only two surviving tribes in Massachusetts, which is, after all, where the white man first got the idea of wiping the Indians out. One of the tribes is the Nipmuck, who can be found on the Hassanamico Indian reservation, Grafton, Massachusetts. The other is the Wampanoag of Gay Head, whose king, Massasoit, made the treaty of friendship with the colonists, and whose son led the revolt against them in 1675 which resulted in the virtual destruction of the tribe. Eagle/Walking Turtle is cagey about what is going on with the Wampanoag these days – but should you be curious you can, apparently, fax them on 508 645-3790.

The countryside near North Adams is refreshingly un-cute. There are hairpin bends up the side of mountain roads, the kind of semi-serious hills you find in the Morvan district of northern Burgundy in France, and the forest doesn't look as if it's just been back-combed. But after we came to Williamstown – a cross between nineteenth-century gothic and Welwyn Garden City – I saw the trees had been at their work again.

The man in the motel was keen to let you know that this was his home too, and his brother or near relation in the French restaurant down the road kept going on about the *confit* of duck being served on a bed of lettuce, and looked at Harry's baseball cap as if he thought it might bite him. Williamstown is a nice place for nice people doing nice things, but even after we bought five T-shirts labelled Williams in large letters, I was glad to get out of there.

As we drove on through rain and green forests, I thought some more about New England and this Puritan business. On the car radio I couldn't get a fundamentalist religious channel. This may have been technical inefficiency on my part, but I still suspect that if there is a guy telling you about the love of Jesus, he will be somewhere at the end of the dial, in response even to my inexpert fingers. The bible in New England is in the people's bones; it is in the rhythms of the poetry, whether it be Frost or Lowell, and its cautions and solutions are behind the looks you get from the traffic cop and the man in the Subs diner. After Williamstown, I abandoned the search for Vermont. Suzan wanted to see Hancock, near Pittsfield, the first Shaker settlement in America. 'You keep going on about this place and the bible,' she said. 'Why not see where it all started?' I said I felt about the Shakers the way I did about the Indians. I thought they were fine but I didn't necessarily want to go and see them.

'Can't we just let them carry on shaking?' I said, as we drove down another narrow twisting road, wet with recent rain. Suzan told me there weren't any Shakers.

'Oh,' said Harry, in the tones of a man who has been cheated; 'you mean it is a *museum*!'

'There'll be working models of Shakers,' said Jack, 'which vibrate when you press a button!'

'It's their actual farm buildings,' said Suzan, 'and the actual barns where they –'

'Had orgies,' said Ned.

She then went on about how the Shakers believed in being simple and true and not having sex, but praising God and leading a good, non-violent life in harmony with God's creatures. This did not encourage Ned or Jack or Harry to go anywhere near a Shaker village, reconstructed or otherwise. But Suzan was determined to go. She told us how they had been started by a woman called Mother Anne Lee from the North of England, who had sought to found a community in which direct instruction from the Word of God was the governing principal. Anybody could get up and report back on their conversation with the Almighty, and they did so, pretty often. 'And they shook!' said Harry. Suzan said that wasn't the point. The point was, she said, they were in touch with something none of us seemed to have any idea about at all – and that was the spiritual.

'The what?' I said.

'The spiritual,' Suzan said, 'the feeling that there is something beyond you and your little concerns!' She went on to tell us that there were a few Shakers surviving up in Maine at Sabbath Day Lake. When Harry said he would like to go to see them, she told him they were 300 miles away. We all realized, I think, that we were going to have to see this museum. There was nothing left to look at but trees anyway. As we drove out of Massachusetts into the more open country of New York State, Suzan was still going on about Shakers. About how they made beautiful furniture that fetched enormous prices at New York sales, and how they were indifferent to money, and helped the poor people from the surrounding villages. She sounded, I thought, like my mother used to sound when she talked about ballet. When I was young, my mother would often force my brothers and me to watch *Coppelia* or the *Sleeping Beauty* on our black-and-white television. We never managed to respond in the correct manner. 'You do not have the kinaesthetic sense!' she would shout, as the four of us sneered at Anton Dolin's codpiece. 'You lack a sense of movement!' It is not only a sense of movement I lack, I told myself grimly, as we followed the long, straight road that led us back into Massachusetts through New York State. I seemed to lack a spiritual dimension as well. Or rather, when I do say something with what I think to be a spiritual insight, it usually seems to be about as profound as the kind of thing found on the inside of a Christmas card. Maybe the Shakers had something to teach me.

In the end I did have a spiritual experience at Hancock Shaker village, Massachusetts, although I am rather ashamed to reveal how it came about. It certainly didn't happen in the cafeteria – the only place in America I went to, apart from the Navajo reservation, that seemed to serve O'Doul's lager. It wasn't the volunteer middle-aged lady at the door or the beautifully-polished table in the meeting room or the black-and-white photographs of old Shakers on the walls, or the Shaker pictures or the Shaker books or the Shaker salt cellars (I am pretty sure they had Shaker salt cellars). It was a television programme. In a small room in the middle of a big, green field in Massachusetts, they were showing a film. I think it may have been made by the BBC. An old lady from Sabbath Day Lake was telling us why she had become a Shaker. She was talking about spirituality, peace and the love of God. I sat, alone, in the darkened room and thought about how far away I was from any of these things. How I didn't believe in her (or anyone else's) God. How I didn't really believe in anything. How, for me, the world is an incomprehensible, foolish, grotesquely cruel place that I don't dare to think about too closely. Because if I did, I might just get to a table with a few chosen friends and sit down and drink myself to death. And as I was thinking all of this, I could see the light of some kind of peace in her face. Although it wasn't the kind of peace I thought I could ever get, I wanted it. Harry came in as I was watching the film.

'Is it any good?' he said.

'It's not bad,' I said. 'It's actually sort of … er … er … moving.'

He moved away nervously.

'I think,' he said, 'I'll go and get a drink.' Spirituality is catching. Once you step into these places – churches, Indian reservations, deserted farms – something comes off the stones, and before you know where you are, you are sitting alone in a darkened room carrying on like Mother Theresa.

When I went out into the pale New England day, Suzan and Ned and Jack and Harry were at a wooden table over in the field. There were horses in the meadow across the way, and further up the slope of the green fields, crops high with the season. In a round, stone barn where once there was a span of horses and a span of cattle, there was a bring-and-buy sale. A fat woman laden with cameras passed me.

'Did you see the Shaker apple corer?' she was saying.

I went across the grass, still wet with rain, towards my family. Mother Ann Lee's church aroused hostility when it first started out, perhaps because of its uncompromising attitude to the notion of the nuclear family. Perhaps Mother Ann's disastrous experience of family life (she seems to have had a 'tyrannical' father) had led her to the Shaker way of life. The buildings, I thought, had the air of an expensive private boarding school. There are times when all or some of the members of any family must long for a clean, white building in the middle of nowhere,

where everything is done at the appointed time. No Mum or Dad, but elders and eldresses. No arguments between brothers and sisters, Hancock bishoprics or the Head of Influence or the East Farm or the Church Farm or the office deacon or the kitchen deaconess who was in charge of brooms, seeds, chairs, etc. But for me the family is preferable to any boarding school. I remember my father asking me when I was eight if I would like to go away to boarding school. 'No,' I said, 'I like it here.' He raised his eyebrows then. 'Do you?' he said. 'How extraordinary!'

I like it here, I thought, as I sat next to Harry, whose baseball cap – perhaps in deference to his situation – was placed firmly and squarely on the top of his head. He was munching a hamburger thoughtfully. People say he looks like me. When I say 'Yes, he's good-looking, don't you think?' they tend to smile and look away. But I like the way he looks. I like the way he eats, too. He was chewing his way now through this giant burger, like a beaver in the early stages of dam development. Soon his cheeks would lean left, and he would nibble surreptitiously at the south-west face of the bread and meat. Then he would swoop up like a helicopter to the north-east corner and take a radical chomp at it. Then panic would suddenly cloud his big blue eyes. *Is there enough ketchup?* A quick, furtive look at his brothers to make sure they hadn't stolen it, and then a huge, red, blisterous blob on the central plateau. Another look round like a wild animal to make sure no one was creeping up behind him and trying to nick his baseball hat. Then more chewing.

I sat next to him and put my arms round him. He continued to eat. To my surprise I found I was singing the Shaker song.

> 'Tis a gift to be simple
> 'Tis a gift to be true.

He looked up at me, quickly.
'Is it?' he said.
'Is it what?' I said.
'Is it good to be simple?' said Harry.
While I thought about this, he chewed some more. Jack said he thought it was a good idea to be devious. 'Credit card fraud is

wrong,' he said, beating the table suddenly, 'but it puts food on the table.' I gave Harry's question some thought. Eventually I said, 'I think it can be good to be simple. But I don't think we should be too frightened of being complicated.'

Ned yawned.

'There he goes again,' he said, 'copping out.'

And then the five of us got up and wandered over the grass to the big white Lincoln Continental.

16

New York New York, New York New York

I drove into New York City in my white Lincoln Continental.

Just writing that sentence has given me a sense of quiet pride. It wasn't, of course, as simple as that. But it's certainly better than writing: 'I hung around Kennedy Airport in my white Lincoln Continental waiting for a limousine to pick me up, and when it didn't I decided to drive into New York, even though I was wetting myself in fear of the prospect.' It's shorter too.

Neither sentence, of course, really does justice to what happened. For a while, out at the airport, we drove along a tangle of freeways and then, suddenly, from over the brow of a hill, I saw a central nest of skyscrapers that wasn't like any other city I had seen in America.

But what one forgets about New York is that it is an architectural landmark. Its tall towers and glass and too-solid concrete landscape and the individual nature of the buildings themselves are as personal as an autograph. Although from a distance it seems like a symbol of modernity, it is a modernity that has only succeeded in not going out of style. Like a stylish black-and-white photograph, New York City is dated and glories in the fact. New York, unlike Athens, Sienna or Prague, was built for the purpose for which it is used. Its manner has been grafted onto almost every other city in Europe – often at the expense of environmental decency – because it is thought to be the quintessential up-to-date city. And yet as its towers rose above me, like the mountains of some giant canyon, as the freeway lined with concrete brought us down into the mid-town tunnel, the things I thought of were age and empire and the terrible authority of the gothic. In the distance, too, it had sparkled like other cities. There was the sea all around it (Manhattan is an island, Suzan was saying from the passenger seat), and there was sunshine and sky as bright as I remembered in San Francisco. But when the tunnel spewed us up, we found ourselves on the floor of a dark, colossal forest.

Here, at the root of these monstrous growths, it was impossible to see how high they grew, or whether the dark had suddenly come upon us because of a cloud crossing the sun or because the concrete cliffs themselves went up so far that, somewhere up above our heads, they arched over towards each other, foreheads kissing on the narrow avenues, blocking out light from the sidewalk.

And then, suddenly, we were turning right into something that I now think must have been Third Avenue, but at the time was nothing like an avenue or even a boulevard. It made the streets laid out by Haussmann in Paris look like a tired re-working of Louis XIV's grand manner. It made Los Angeles' efforts at thoroughfares look like an over-ambitious second draft of the Périphérique or the North Circular. It was certainly well beyond being a lane or a highway, and whatever it was, it was not a road.

It made me think, for some reason, of brass bands and ticker tape and drum majorettes, and ridiculous optimism. The sun – there was sun here – picked out the light from the windows, shone on the yellow taxis. The people – there were all of a sudden a great many people – all seemed to be in a hurry. Except that they were being drawn along this enormous avenue by some magnetic field, or answering the call of the hidden god of the place.

Whoever He was, I decided, after the briefest of glances at some of the passing faces, He was something to do with money. And (the sun had gone behind a cloud now) He was angry about something. Maybe they weren't working hard enough. Maybe He wanted higher buildings. Maybe He had suddenly noticed that there were potholes in the road and that His People were having the wrong kind of fun in His petrified forest.

Ahead of us, a girl on roller-blades hung onto the back of a yellow taxi. She was about nineteen or twenty, had a small, nylon ruck-sack on her back, and as she swooped through the traffic, she turned aside with the sweetest of smiles to a passing motorist, laying her index finger to her lips, as if to say, 'Don't tell! Please don't tell!'

Then we were headed left and over to our right was a thing that could have been a museum but turned out to be Grand Central Station (or was it the New York Public Library?); whatever it was, although it was only a measly couple of hundred feet high, it was built like a wrestler and wore its glass and stone and metal like a badge of power. Everything was moving in the same direction very fast. That made it feel as if you had fallen into a river. But not an English stream – something as powerful as the Hudson, even now hauling itself down past Manhattan from the green, mist-wrapped spaces of New York State.

'They're all one way!' Suzan was yelling. 'You just get on one street and follow it along. They all go north or south!'

The boys had dropped their Walkmans, and Ned, picking up his copy of *Seven Types of Ambiguity*, held it up against the place as if to ward off an evil spirit.

'It is,' he said, 'rather amazing.'

This from Ned is very high praise indeed.

'It's more than amazing!' I said. I found that I too was shouting: 'It's fantastic! It's phenomenal! It's incredible! It's New York!' Harry, picking up the tone of this, started to jump up and down on his feet.

'New Yawk!' he sang. 'New Yawk, New Yawk, New Yawk!' And in this manner we turned into Madison Avenue.

One of these buildings was presumably the Empire State Building, but for all I knew they could all be the Empire State Building. At each intersection groups of pedestrians waited, then surged forward – but although I had seen all this many times before on the movies, I had a revelatory sense of how small the cinema makes things. How unfairly it guides the eye to its chosen target. The people in the films, from *Manhattan* to *The French Connection*, always seemed to dominate the frame. But now I could see that, in more than any other city I could name, architecture was the dominating presence. These curiously indi-

170

vidual hanks of rock, these sheer faces studded with eyes, were the governing principle of a city so grand I could hardly believe the island of Manhattan could support its weight.

The logic of the streets often compounds the spirit of the place. West 44th Street, West 45th Street, West 46th Street, climbing in idiot progression, helping to preserve the illusion that we, too, were going up – language and number pushing us up like toothpaste in a tube – up towards the park and Harlem! One straight line! All the way from the East Village to the latitude of the Triborough Bridge! New York is a living mass – a place designed to be read at a glance. Like some deserted ancient monument, occupied by gypsies who have no understanding of its culture, it is all too obviously much *more* than the people it is designed to serve. It towers over the visitor, declaring itself with an authority I have seen in no other city.

'Go left!' yelled Suzan.

She seemed suddenly very cheerful.

'It's great!' she went on. 'You go left and then you go right! It's all one-way. The streets just go up and up, one way! If that … ' she continued staring at the map on her knees, ' … if that was Fourth Avenue then this, turn left, is Fifth Avenue!'

And lo and behold it was. And at the corner of Fifth Avenue and West 55th Street was the Peninsula Hotel.

I had booked the Peninsula Hotel in the spirit of a man who feels his days on the planet are numbered. We were staying in upstate New York at a place called the Bear Mountain Inn, run by the same men in wide hats who have taken over Yosemite. The fire alarm went off three times in the night, as well as a device that was only supposed to go off when an earthquake or imminent nuclear attack had been announced. We had spent most of the night standing out under the stars with a lot of other people in dressing gowns. That was perhaps why I decided to book us into the most expensive hotel I could find in New York City.

'We've stayed too long,' I said, 'in crappy motels. For the last three days we are going to spend, spend, spend!'

'How much', said Suzan, 'are we going to spend, spend, spend?'

When I started to look at the prices, I realized that the most we could afford to spend, spend, spend was at the Peninsula Hotel. And even then I wasn't sure we would be able to sleep all night in the place. The guidebook said it was built in 1905, and was the home of the one-time Maxine's club and often played host to visiting movie stars. At its rooftop bar in the early evening, they said, you could see all the most successful people in mid-town Manhattan. I could not easily see us fitting into this grouping, but when a man is determined to spend money it is useless to try and stop him. There was a rooftop health bar and a health suite. There were saunas and jacuzzis and exercise machines, and a heated swimming pool, and many other things that Ned, Jack, Harry, Suzan and I had not seen since California.

'We won't tell them,' said Suzan, when I had done a series of calculations and worked out that we could just about afford three nights in the place. 'We'll tell them we're staying somewhere really gross.' Which is perhaps why they nearly hid on the floor when we drew up outside a heavily-sculpted, mock-gothic façade just off Fifth Avenue and two men in red hats and gold coats leapt forward to open the doors of the car.

'Could you park this car for me?' I said.

Park the bleeding car yourself, is what I would have responded. But the man seemed to eat up this treatment.

'Certainly, sir,' he said. 'Is it a hire car?'

'Hertz!' I said.

'No problem!' said the man in the red hat and gold coat. I'm almost sure he clicked his heels. I dug in my pocket and pulled out a wad of dollars. This seemed to please him.

'Just got in, sir?' he said.

'Yes,' I said, 'from Texas.'

I don't know why I said this. Perhaps I'd only just realized I was wearing the black stetson hat I had bought on the Navajo reservation. Not only that, I was still in the hiking boots, the Marks & Spencer shorts and a grubby T-shirt. From the car came piles of dirty knickers, Kachina dolls wrapped in newspaper, six assorted jumpers, five pairs of trousers, three pairs of swimming trunks, a large string bag containing the *Truth of a Hopi*, *David*

Copperfield, the *Collected Poems of John Masefield*, *Three Men in a Boat* by Jerome K. Jerome, *Seven Types of Ambiguity* by William Empson, *Death of a Naturalist* by Seamus Heaney, Plato's *Republic*, the *Collected Poems of John Cleveland* and *The Lost Continent* by Bill Bryson. There also came five pairs of socks, four glasses, and an Ibanez electric guitar purchased from a music store in Santa Barbara, California, eight CDs of Black Sabbath, a D, a G and an E blues harmonica, a piece of rock from the Grand Canyon, a heavy-duty torch, twenty-four packets of sugar and thirty sachets of shampoo and shower gel from, among other places, the Holiday Inn, Monterey, Caesar's Palace, Las Vegas and the Mondrian Hotel, Los Angeles. There also came six pairs of boxer shorts, two bottles of Californian wine, three bottles of fruit juice, a half-eaten pizza that had been bought somewhere between Amherst, Massachusetts and New Haven, Connecticut. There also came four pairs of sneakers, six pairs of tights and a Los Angeles Raiders T-shirt.

Some of these things were in suitcases. Some of them were not. But I didn't care. I was a different man from the character who had cowered in front of Caesar's Palace about a week earlier. 'My money,' I said to myself in a Texan accent, 'is as good as any of yourn!' I had to make a strong effort to stop myself from calling hotel employees 'boy'. Suzan, who was wearing her white stetson with something of my confidence, seemed to have adopted the same tactic. The men in gold coats and red hats carried our possessions proudly through to the lobby in the Peninsula Hotel and piled them just in front of the desk. There seemed, as far as I could see, to be no other people with luggage in the marbled foyer of the place. I jammed my black stetson onto my head, and walked with the deliberate tread of a hick with money towards the desk. 'Do you want to see my credit card?' I said. The desk clerk seemed unphased by the fact that her lobby had started to look like a car boot sale.

In fact everyone at the Peninsula Hotel seemed curiously glad to see us. What I didn't understand about their manner was that they managed to suggest that this was not simply to do with the fact that each room would cost $250 a night. And that was before

Ned, Jack and Harry started on the mini-bar. I think what it meant was that most of the people who use the place have so much money that it really doesn't matter. I looked once again at the concierge. Her manners were as exquisite as a geisha's. She managed to give the impression not only that she approved of us, but that for some reason of her own she almost quite liked us. She might almost prefer to be us than herself. She took us up in the lift, took us to our room, explained how the lights could be turned on from the telephone, and dealt with charm and style with Harry's enquiries as to the whereabouts of the jacuzzi. Finally she wished us a pleasant stay in New York City.

I had noticed quite early on that there was a distinct relation in America between the quality of people's smiles and the money you paid them. In the restaurant of the Chatham Bars Inn, Massachusetts, I had watched a young woman's shy grin turned into a wide gape of ecstatic pleasure as I wrote $10 in the space marked 'gratuity' on the credit card slip. But in the concierge's case there was no sign that cash was the point of the relationship between us. You would have thought, from the way she was carrying on about the health suite, the rooftop juice bar, the bidet and the designer pillowcases, that they were all free.

When she had gone and Ned and Jack and Harry retreated to their own quarters, Suzan and I went to the window. Down on Fifth Avenue in the gathering darkness, yellow taxis were strung out like beads. In the doorway of a tiny church, squashed between two skyscrapers, an old man in ragged clothes was climbing into a cardboard box.

'Did you know,' I said to Suzan, 'that there are more murders in New York City than in … '

'I don't want to hear,' she said.

She went back and sat on the bed.

'I'll tell you another thing,' she said. 'I could do without that guy in the cardboard box.'

We went out to the street where one of the men in red-and-gold uniforms hailed us a taxi. If I stayed too long at the Peninsula Hotel, I decided, I might need help in brushing my teeth or getting my shoes on in the morning. Its hospitality was insidious. Just when you were on your way through a room, heading for somewhere that was nowhere very much, a man dressed as if for a society wedding would leap out at you from behind a pillar and, often using your full name, wish you the compliments of the season. When I walked out onto West 55th Street, I had the strong urge to go back in through the doors and come out again – just in case any of the passers-by had missed out on the fact that I was staying in a hotel that cost $250 a night.

When I got into the front seat of the yellow taxi, even though the driver looked as if he had just been sleeping rough in the Ukraine, I was still touched by glamour, not quite human. The man next to me might be telling me that he had arrived in New York three months ago, had no money and lived in one room in Brooklyn, but I was an extra in a brochure. I was as unreal as the amount of money I was going to have to fork out in about sixty-two hours from now. When I asked the driver later how he got into the country, he said he used his brother's passport. Was there any problem with this? He said not at all. Quite a lot of people did it. He said he spent most of his time in New York with other Russians. 'And buy green card!' he said. The price of a green card was exorbitant. But after you got a green card, then it was possible to become a citizen. I could not imagine having a similar conversation with a mini-cab driver in London. 'I am an illegal immigrant from Bangladesh. I got in on my brother's passport.' It's natural to want to be in America. It's the most natural thing in the world. And if the law tries to stop you, well, who makes the law? Is it such a good law? This question of the law is at the root of the American attitude to violence. The statistics tell their own story. But what they don't tell you is what it's like to be there. Sacramento, curiously one of the most violent cities in the whole of the US, seems on the surface to be deeply ordinary. An acquaintance of mine who made a film among criminals there told me that the violence is as casual and as ordinary as the city itself. The violence, like so many other things in the country, comes from preserving basic human rights. The right to abuse yourself and others with drugs, the right to buy a gun, the right to use it. All these are part of your right to be an American in your own way. Nobody hides behind their office in America – not even the President. The separation of function and individual enshrined in the law pervades every aspect of life.

The next morning we took another taxi. This time it was driven by a man called (I think) Gopal. His picture was hanging on the dashboard in front of me. It did not inspire confidence. He looked, I thought, like a composite photofit of almost every international terrorist whose picture has ever appeared in the English papers. When I stole a glance left and took a look at him he looked even more sinister. 'GOPAL' – NOT HIS REAL NAME – IS WANTED IN CONNECTION WITH THE MURDER OF AN ENGLISH FAMILY ON VACATION IN NEW YORK!

'I'd like to go to the Statue of Liberty!' I said to him as we pulled out on to Fifth Avenue. He did not respond. It was possible, I decided, that the man spoke no English at all. How, in that case, had he managed to get all the way from Bangladesh or the Sudan or wherever he was from, get himself a driving licence, a yellow cab and, presumably, somewhere to stay?

Just when I had given up all hope of hearing the sound of his voice, he said – 'New York is very bad place!'

I said I thought it seemed very nice. Gopal said it was nice if you enjoyed people shoving revolvers in your face and demanding money. I said that hadn't happened to me yet. Gopal said that it would. I said I was only staying three days. Gopal said that in that case I might just be lucky. He advised me to get out while I was ahead.

'People here,' he said, 'only interested money. I have friend coming from Bombay. He only interested money.'

I said I thought that was sad. He said it was. He added that his friend – who had arrived with nothing – was now a millionaire. This, said Gopal, was the positive side of New York. Either you got revolvers stuck in your face or you made a million bucks.

'Which kind you think I am?' he said.

I was warming to Gopal. But I did not give him an entirely truthful answer.

'I think,' I said, 'you may well get lucky!'

He grinned then. He had the worst teeth of anyone I have ever met in my life. He went on to tell me that if I wanted to see the Statue of Liberty he would take me to a place called the Battery, at the South end of Manhattan. There was a boat that took you out there, he said.

'But,' he went on, 'Statue of Liberty … piecea shit.'

He pronounced this as if he had just read it in a book of useful colloquial phrases. I said this wasn't what I had heard.

'Statue of Liberty … ' went on Gopal, driving at about forty miles an hour towards a brick wall, ' … all queues … many people … Ellis Island where people come immigrants also piecea shit on account people.'

He was obviously a man who knew his way around. I asked him where we were. He gestured over his shoulder and said 'Greenwich Village.' From the back I heard Suzan asking me what he was saying.

'He says there are too many people trying to see the Statue of Liberty!' I said.

'And what does he suggest?' said Suzan.

Gopal suggested we go on something called the Circle Line. Harry said he didn't want to go on the underground. People got mugged on the underground, he said. Gopal said the Circle Line was a boat.

'Go all round Manhattan Island!' he said. 'Four hours. Good.'

This, from Gopal, was praise indeed. And so it was that we found ourselves boarding a boat from a quay on the West Side. It wasn't a very big boat – about the size of the kind of ferry you find in the Hebrides – but its atmosphere was seriously naval. Our tour guide wore white drill shorts, a white shirt and a fetching peaked cap, decorated with gold braid. As we steamed out into the open water, Harry said –

'We're on the sea!'

Although, technically speaking, we were on the Hudson river, I knew what he meant. The New Jersey shore, opposite us, had that distant, magical quality I always associate with a land mass coming into view from the ocean. And, as we headed towards Liberty Island, the gigantic towers around the World Trade Centre at the southern tip of Manhattan reared up in the sunlight, as entrancingly as the first pilgrim's landfall. We crowded at the bow of the boat as we swung round by the Statue of Liberty and back up towards the East River.

I decided, afterwards, that Gopal had it right. The Statue of Liberty is one of those monuments that resembles its reproduced image too closely to be really surprising. But, from a steamer, ploughing across the mouth of the Hudson, it acquires romance. In fact, as we headed up the East River under the Queensboro Bridge, the whole island of Manhattan was transformed into a spectacle for our benefit. There was traffic, curiously absorbed with itself in the glittering day, there was a grim-looking public park, and, beyond the Brooklyn Bridge, past the conflicting currents of Hellgate and through the narrow channel of the Harlem River that brings you back into the main current of the Hudson, there were high cliffs of rock studded with more of those unforgiving New England trees. From the water I understood the city for the first time. It is nothing like the country or the cities around it. And although, up by Columbia University at the northern tip of the island, it is separated from the rest of America by a sheet of water you feel you could swim across, Manhattan is as isolated in Puritan New England as a vessel from Mars that put down, by accident, in the middle of a Kansas cornfield.

It seemed to me, as we rounded the corner into the Hudson river, as if Manhattan was ready to be cut adrift and to float out into the glittering Atlantic like the liners tethered to her West Side.

When we got back to the city, Harry said he wanted to climb the Empire State Building. Ned said he would be advised to use the lift. We took another cab – this time driven by a man called Jurgens who looked as if he had worked in the supply department of the Baader Meinhof gang. I tried to get him to talk but he was chary about saying where he came from. It was possible, I thought, that he came from some illegal sub-department of the former Soviet Union. Out there in the hills of the Caucasus there is probably a place with its own language and government, entirely devoted to turning out New York cab drivers. He seemed pretty vague about where the Empire State Building might be but, when I thrust our tourist map into his face, he seemed to recognize it. The landmark that clinched it for him, for some reason, was the New York Public Library.

We joined the queue for the Empire State Building. It begins, unpromisingly, in an Art Deco foyer, full of office workers. But, after you have negotiated two lifts and you are looking down at the packed squares, the Brill Building, the World Trade Centre, the Chrysler Building shining like a new metal toy in the August day, you feel once again the simple thrill of being *above* something so huge in scale.

Jack and I stood looking down at the city.

'One day,' he said, 'when I am grown up and eat coleslaw and go to art galleries I will probably understand all this. But right now I am confused.'

I said I was confused too. I said I thought America was a place designed to confuse people like us. A gigantic landmass where, for the last three or four hundred years, people have made up their own history and made grand gestures and then felt the need to expand on them.

'It's been good though, hasn't it?' he said.

'Yes,' I said.

He looked across at Ned, who was gazing down at Central Park.

'He's been quite good, considering,' he said.

'I think so,' I said.

'And Harry hasn't been too annoying!'

'No,' I said.

He looked at me quizzically. I thought – *he'll be sixteen soon. And then, like Ned, he'll want to be off on his own. And I don't want to stop that. Except sometimes I do. I want time to stand still and all five of us be frozen there, the way we were high above New York City, lucky and happy and lit by the summer sun.*

'Come on, Frogspawn,' he said, 'we have much tourism to complete.'

Journeys, I thought, as we headed towards the lifts, *are as much about your travelling companions as they are about the places you visit.*

We went to the Upper West Side and the Lower East Side, and the Battery and the Garment District. We went on a subway (which seemed clean and decorous compared with the London Underground), on a shiny blue bus up to Harlem, and drove in three cabs where the drivers spoke no English at all. We got lost on our way to the Metropolitan Museum of Art, and when we got inside it we got lost again. We were offered fake Rolex watches and three different kinds of mood-altering drug. We took cocktails on the roof of the Peninsula Hotel, and Chinese food near Canal Street.

But at night in the Peninsula Hotel, I could be heard adding up the amount we were spending. In the jacuzzi nearly twenty storeys up, cradled in warm water among the topmost boughs of Fifth Avenue, I was to be seen counting on my fingers as I tried to work out how many television plays I would have to write before I could make it square with the management.

It was time to go. On a bright afternoon we took a limousine out to the airport. As we sat on a 747 waiting for take-off, Suzan leaned across to me –

'You're going to write a book about this, aren't you?'

'Yes,' I said.

She looked out of the window. The flight didn't seem to make her nervous at all. She's changed, I thought. America has changed her. When she turned back to me she spoke slowly and seriously.

'What's it going to be called?'

'From Wimbledon to Waco,' I said.

She yawned.

'We don't live in Wimbledon,' she said, 'and we never got to Waco. Waco is in Texas, isn't it?'

'I know,' I said, 'but I like the title … '

The pilot's reassuring English voice told us we were number three in the queue for take-off. He manoeuvred the plane, as clumsy as a swan on land, out along the tarmac. How will England be, I thought to myself, will it be small and mean-looking? Or will it welcome me the way home is supposed to? I realized how completely America had blotted out the place where I was born and where I had lived for the first forty-six years of my life.

'It'll be the usual thing,' Suzan said. 'Few jokes and a bit of scenery.'

'Yes,' I said.

'The thing is,' she said, 'people read this stuff and think this is what we're really like. Unbelievable though it may seem. And they have no idea. Not really.'

'No,' I said.

'We're not like that,' she said. 'Are we?' I closed my hand over hers.

'No,' I said. 'Of course we're not.'